Crushed

Crushed

My NHS Summer

Jan McCourt

Published by
The University of Buckingham Press
Yeomanry House
Hunter Street
Buckingham MK18 1EG

© Jan McCourt

ISBN 9781908684196

First Published as an E-Book on Amazon Version (1)
2012.04

Northfield Farm Publishing
Northfield Farm
Whissendine Lane
Cold Overton
Oakham, Rutland
LE15 7QF

www.northfieldfarmpublishing.com
See also:
www.northfieldfarm.com
blog.northfieldfarm.com

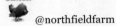

@northfieldfarm

This edition: Version (2) 2012.05
Printed in Great Britain on
recycled paper

Editor: Dominic McCourt
Graphic Design: Charlotte McCourt

Contents

This book is dedicated to:

All the wonderful people, from that field to The Leicester Royal Infirmary who scraped me up, smiled, laughed, listened and then stuck me back together and cared for me directly.

To those who cared for me indirectly by holding my life together outside hospital to give me something to return to.

My children.

<u>Front Cover</u>: Jan with two of the Police helicopter team who airlifted him from the field at Northfield Farm.

<u>Back Cover</u>: Jan standing for the first time. (Photo: Mike Wilford)

"Night time freezes blackness into giant fears, demonblack, held by the tail."

Christy Nolan

If hospital staffing could just take these words into account, maybe there would be less pain and trauma at night, which would result in shorter, happier stays and lower costs.

Prologue

Jan McCourt, well known Investment Banker turned Farmer, returned to his grassland farm on the picturesque border dividing Leicestershire from Rutland after a week-end of work at a music festival.

By the end of that day, he was fighting for his life in A&E in The Leicester Royal Infirmary.

This is the story, in truly graphic detail, of his extraordinary experience.

At times horrific, at times hilarious, it is a story of agony and of a true miracle.

It is also a story of the wonders of the British National Health Service as well as of a few of its horrors. It is a story of pride and of shame.

It is a story which should be read by those who have given up hope, by victims of accidents, their families, and by every employee of the NHS.

Humpty Dumpty sat on a wall, Humpty Dumpty had a great fall

I decided to write what follows just a few days after my accident, although I was unable to actually start writing for many months. I realise only now that that decision was also part of what helped me survive. I had then, and, as I continue to write, still have, no clear vision of where it might lead or even really what form it should take.

Light a bomb

I only knew that I wanted to share something of what I was learning. Not so much to share the personal horror of what happened, as to ignite a bit of a bomb under the constantly negative carping about the NHS. To show a little of what the Consultants, rising young Doctors, Nurses, Tea Ladies and Cleaners, not to mention the patients, are all up against. I also wanted to show what miracles can be achieved, when all these people work together.

Paying tribute

Above all I wanted to pay tribute to the extra-ordinary collection of people who gave so much and worked so hard to put me back together again. Maybe in doing so, I would raise a few eyebrows by not holding back on some of the less pleasant details. Perhaps I would stir a little debate. If so, so much the better.

Why write?

I suspect that most introductions are written either during or after the creation of the work they are introducing. This one is no different.

In truth, I first conceived of writing this for myself. I felt that it would be an essential part of my eventual recovery. Senior Staff Nurse Dylan (sorry if I have the title wrong) told me on more than one occasion;

Mind and emotions

"Jan, we are here to do the best job of putting you back together we can. But that is not just a question of seeing that your bones knit back together and that we get you walking and healed physically. We are here to help you to heal your mind and your emotions."

Healing

Dylan and his colleagues of all ranks are wiser than they may realise. Rarely do any of them actually do the healing. The individual heals his or her own self. These great people stick you back together and then show you how to heal, and support you on the way.

Starting to write

Actually starting to write was incredibly difficult. I tried while in hospital, my head bursting with words and ideas, but dried up as soon as I put pen to paper. Using a laptop was too painful, no matter how I tried. I couldn't sit up for weeks and I couldn't support the weight of a lap top. So that too was abandoned. I tried a Dictaphone, but that lay largely unused, though I did make one short, haunting recording in which I tried to describe the pain I was in. I tried again and again once I had returned home, only to fail.

Italy

Eventually I took a three week break in Italy, a tiny ancient one room studio in glorious Umbria, where I slept and woke at strange hours and managed to write most of what follows.

Telling this tale was part of the process of healing. One of the hardest things to portray was the pain. I was fearful of creating a narrative which would be let down by repetitive unimaginative attempts to describe the physical challenge presented by Pain.

Kicking the drugs

When I arrived in Italy I was taking 24 pills every day to fight the pain. I hated taking them, and despised myself for relying on them, so I started to reduce the number. There followed days, and especially nights, of cold sweats, hot sweats and imaginary spiders crawling up and down my legs.

The late Christy Nolan wrote of Kerry in his autobiography. I paraphrase it here:

"Night time freezes blackness into giant fears, demonblack, held by the tail."

For me, and I am sure for so many others, night-time in these circumstances is no respecter of the clock or even the light. I managed to reduce my pill count from twenty-four to three.

Together again!

Despite what you might anticipate, this modest work is not an 'exposé' in the sense that you will not find in these pages great and terrible revelations of the dreadful things which happen within the NHS. It does touch upon certain problems and I am sure that proper investigation would reveal many more.

No, it is an exclamation of joy, at what was and can be achieved. If the descriptions are a little too close to the bone (excuse the pun), a little too distressing in their detail, I make no apology as, without their intimacy, the narrative would have no value. If my work finds favour, fantastic. If not, so be it, it will have achieved its primary aim of helping to put this particular Humpty Dumpty back together again.

Air Ambulance

My accident happened in the middle of a field. Access to the location is narrow, uneven and circuitous. What is known as 'The Golden Hour' is the key time within which medical treatment has the greatest chance of saving a life. It applies to any medical emergency. Until my accident, I knew very little about the Air Ambulance service. I had no idea, for example that all the regional services are entirely privately funded. I was actually rescued by a Police Service helicopter which just happened to be close enough, with enough fuel to help. These guys can be chasing a criminal one minute and saving lives the next.

A proportion of all proceeds from this book will go to Air Ambulance Services.

Jan McCourt
Northfield Farm
Rutland/Leicestershire
England   May 2012

Chapter One –

Going Home

It was a Monday afternoon. I had spent the weekend and the end of the previous week down in Surrey with my catering wagon selling burgers, bacon and sausages from early in the morning until midnight. The weather had been brilliant, the music good, the girls very pretty, and business terrific.

As I drove into the yard at home, the sun was still shining. Everyone seemed to have gone home. I parked up and locked the trailer and car. I walked into the house, poured myself a long cool drink of juice from the fridge and went and lay down on the front lawn to catch the last of the sun. After half an hour or so, I got up, stretched and decided to go for a walk.

I went out into the yard and across into the back field. The grass was parched and the ground as hard as rock, but I felt more alive than I had in ages. My boys were with their mother and I was looking forward to a quiet night before resuming the delightful chaos that always accompanies them wherever they go, after they came back to me the next day.

The tractor

My tractor was making its way steadily across the field, hay mower attached behind it, topping the weeds that are the inevitable result of farming without the use of sprays. My friend, a self-employed contractor, was driving it. He appeared to have seen me, I waved and headed across to a spot at which I guessed he might halt. As I walked across, he swung the tractor around and came to a halt just before the brow of the hill, about twenty or thirty yards ahead and slightly downhill of me. I adjusted my approach accordingly and arrived just as he alighted from the tractor. We shook hands and discussed each other's weekend.

Crushed

A funny noise

Rather than get back in, he went around to the back of the tractor and bent down to peer underneath the mower which was suspended, slightly offset to one side, behind the tractor, saying that he had heard a strange noise. I came across to stand directly behind the middle of the back of the tractor and kneeled down to see if I could help. I was on my hands and knees, stretched forwards, craning my neck to see under the mower.

The tractor moved

The tractor moved silently backwards.

My life seemed to switch into slow motion.

I called out to warn him that the tractor was moving on us. He did not move, and for some reason, neither did I. I called to him a second time to get out from under the mower. Whether he had heard me or not the first time, I do not know, but he started to move after I had shouted again. I then began to move to escape also. All sorts of strange thoughts passed through my head. I seemed only to be able to move terribly slowly. A list of ways in which I might be crushed crossed my mind, each one paralyzing me from doing anything at all. After dismissing the thought of lying flat between the wheels in the hope of the tractor passing clean over me, I started to roll to my right. For some reason I was unable to simply spring to my feet. I had rolled round to a sitting position, my legs stretched out in front of me on the ground, when the left hand rear wheel of the tractor touched my back. It all still seemed to be happening ever so slowly.

I was stuck

I felt the weight of the wheel begin to press against my spine. It started to push me forward. I was in a dream. This could not really be happening to me. I pushed back, but the huge force of the tractor, its rear wheels ballasted with water, just kept coming. It pushed me relentlessly forward. My legs started to stretch out straighter on the ground before me. I woke up only to find that I was already awake. The dream-like, wading through mud-like, feeling of the previous moments had gone, the horror of what was happening, no longer a dream, roared in my face. I screamed back at it. I was stuck. There was nothing I could do. The wheel pushed inexorably on.

The top part of my body bent forward, I started to shout or scream, no doubt both. I am still not sure whether the fear or pain was more terrible. The wheel seemed to want to climb up onto my back. I realised that I was being folded in two, that the tractor was first going to crush my hips and pelvis, then follow directly up the line of my spine and squash it down between my legs before rolling on over my head at which point I would eventually know no more.

Crack!

I felt the first bones begin to crack. The tractor concentrated its weight in one spot. The middle of my lower back felt the pressure, and the back of my pelvis gave way like balsa wood. First one hip broke and then, very quickly, the front of my pelvis at the top inside of each leg snapped clean through. As the wheel advanced, my head was forced ever closer towards the parched hard earth. I continued to shout and scream. I even called upon God. I was certain, I knew, that I was dying, and yet I was still stunned with disbelief that this was really happening. The wheel kept pressing, now at the base of my spine, and just as I gave up all hope, the wheel stopped.

Release

The shock, the pain, and my own screaming all mixed into one ball of fire which was destroying me in its intense heat. I could sense the driver coming round to the wheel, calling to me. I felt the wheel roll back away from me, the pressure lifting, the pain still mounting. He called to me to try to get out while he used all his strength to move the machine off me. You read from time to time about brief manifestations of superhuman strength, such as a Mother lifting the full weight of a car off a child. Although my friend later denied it, there is no other explanation as to how one man could push a seven tonne tractor up a hill, even only a very short distance.

He put his hands and shoulder to the wheel of the tractor and pushed with all his might. Somehow, I made one more turn onto my front, the tractor eased back and settled onto the space where it had pinned me down. My right arm was resting so close, almost touching the wall of the tractor tyre.

Memory of smiles

He was down on his knees by my head talking to me. Then for a brief moment he lost it. He talked to himself, he talked to me. He froze, perhaps just as I had frozen as the tractor bore down on me. A tiny moment of time ago, we had been all smiles, happy in the beauty of the early evening sun. Now we were plunged into a nightmare from which I might never emerge.

999

I begged him to call 999 and he snapped out of it, seemed to focus again, and pulled out his phone. I continued to make a terrible noise. In between speaking to the emergency services, giving details of what had happened and where we were, he gently but firmly told me to breathe deeply, and reassured me that I would be alright.

While he spoke on the phone, in my brief moments of lucidity, I tried to work out just what I had damaged. My whole body was in spasm. I tried to move but reeled with the pain. I was determined to know whether I could still move my feet. I managed to move my head enough to just see the tips of my toes.

Movement

I moved them, they moved. Only a tiny movement, but enough to convince me that my spine was intact. The pain seemed to ease a little. I told him what I thought I had broken. Uncannily accurate as it turned out later. Then it really hit me, wave after wave of searing, bright, vile pain the like of which I had never known. Death seemed to be looming over me and no matter how deeply I tried to breathe, its cold hands moved agonizingly up my body.

Vile, Dark Pain

I closed my eyes and prayed to pass out. This was no gentle passing, no sweet smells, no music, and no light. Only the intense, vile, dark, pain, my friend's desperate voice as he called first the emergency services and then his wife to get her to come over to guide the ambulance to the remote spot where we were. I wanted it gone, I was giving up. It was just too much to expect me to hold on. I was going, the pain would soon surely ease and disappear. I could not go on.

My children

The faces of my three children appeared before me. A younger version of my fourteen year old daughter, who rarely spoke to me now, smiled and laughed. Her impudent voice called me back, her big, sparkling eyes begging me to stay. My boys, younger, but somehow even stronger, entreated me also, telling me I had to be strong and stay. The thought of history repeating itself and me deserting them, by dying, as my father had left me, shimmered across my view. I could not do it, I had to live. I had to stay awake and fight for as long as I possibly could. I reached out for the pain. I sucked it in and embraced it, riding each huge wave which sought to send me tumbling into the darkness. I fought the biggest battle of my life while all the time the three faces watched me and gave me the strength to carry on.

Chapter Two –

Living Hell

Despite the living hell, the emergency services seemed to arrive pretty quickly, though how long it actually took them, I don't know. They arrived in force though. Ambulance, fire engine and police. They all formed a circle around me, one or other of them talking constantly to me. Reassuring me, keeping me awake and asking me questions. Everyone seemed to be talking into radios or phones. My friend's wife bent down, tears in her eyes and touched my brow, her hands as soothing as her voice, full of concern and emotion. Every face I saw looked as worried as hell. I continued to yell and scream though perhaps not quite as loudly now. I am not sure.

Crushed

Potentially fatal?

There was an exchange between two officials. I heard a voice crackle over a radio asking whether this was a potentially fatal incident. The policeman, I think, being asked the question, answered that it was, and looked horrified as I called out that I had heard them and thanks a bunch. Despite the pain and the stark words, it injected a little humour into the situation, albeit of the blackest kind.

They gave me some oxygen, and explained that they needed to turn me over from my front to my back. I was not in any position to argue, but it was the first of so many occasions when the anticipation was every bit as awful as the reality. Just like in the films, several people gathered around me, each taking part of my body, and firmly but swiftly, and as gently as they could, turned me over. Everything went so dark for a moment. I bunched my eyes tightly shut against the pain, so black and so huge as it tried to suck everything out of me.

Turning me over

Talking all the time, the men explained what they were doing as they turned me first to one side, and then to the other, they slid two boards under me, pushing them toward the centre of my back until with an excruciating series of clicks, the boards locked together. As they started to bind me tightly to the board and fix foam cushions around my head and neck, one of them announced the good news that there was a helicopter on its way to pick me up.

Helicopter

I was still fighting to stay awake. When I heard about the helicopter I thought what a shame it was that my boys could not be there to enjoy the ride. How daft a thought that was. It occurred to me that if the accident did not kill me my rescuers had better be sure that the helicopter did not fly in from beyond wherever my cattle might be standing in the field and, causing a stampede, drive them to crush me under their feet.

The air started to throb

Very quickly it seemed, the air started to throb and the crew covered my head to keep the dust from my eyes and mouth. Dark under the cover, I felt the temptation again to simply drift away. I clung to the pain and life until the dust settled and the cover was lifted. There was lots of talking going on around me but by now I was bound tightly on the board and I could only see whoever or whatever passed immediately in front of my eyes.

Loading me up

Having asked me if I had a preference for a hospital, someone explained that there was only enough light & fuel to take me to The Leicester Royal Infirmary. With that decision made, my board was gently lifted up and carried towards the helicopter. The act of lifting caused all my muscles to tighten even further and the worst pain returned and exploded again with each step that my bearers took. I could see the slowly rotating propeller and feel the turbulence it created as they carried me underneath the tail of the machine and slid me in to what seemed to be a tiny space.

Even sharper burst of pain

For a moment everything went black again as I was pushed into what seemed to be an impossibly small area. I felt the door or doors push hard against my feet as they tried to close them. An even sharper burst of pain. At nearly six foot four inches tall there was not enough room to fit me straight into the back of the helicopter. They pulled the door back open and slid my board across at an angle to close it properly. My head was now back in light alongside the open side door of the helicopter. A paramedic climbed in and over me so that I was staring up in between his legs. I still had an oxygen mask on and was trying to breathe as best I could. The tube from the mask fell across my face and seemed ridiculously disturbing, given all the pain. I could not call out or move to attract the paramedic's attention, but eventually he noticed and gently moved it with a kind smile and soft inaudible words.

Take off

The side door closed, I heard various routines being checked and the bird began to rise, at first with a painful jolt, and then more and more smoothly as we flew away across the farm towards Leicester.

I remember thinking again that my boys would have enjoyed the flight so much more than me.

The flight

The vibrations of the machine were fairly steady so there was no increase in the pain which raged on. Despite this, the pain still caused me to cry out at regular intervals. It was like a succession of waves on a beach, but definitely with the tide coming in. Each wave would crash upon me and then retreat for a brief moment only to return with greater force the next time.

The journey seemed too brief. Like so many journeys, in a way I dreaded it ending because, in the state I was in, any change represented more pain and uncertainty. As if I could not tell, my companion told me that we were approaching our destination. I could feel the whirly bird steady, descend and come to land.

The landing

I think the landing was probably as smooth as was possible, but to me it felt like a massive lurching crash. The doors at my feet opened, air rushed in together with the noise of the dying rotor blades. Kind words were being spoken from all sides to me as I was dragged out of the belly of the machine and onto some sort of trolley (a 'gurney' I think they would call it on ER). I am not sure where I was exactly, but the wheels of my trolley rumbled painfully as I was taken from our landing place into the Accident and Emergency Department of The Leicester Royal Infirmary.

Chapter Three –

Leicester Royal Infirmary

I don't remember much about A&E. I do remember reading a sign which said 'Resuscitation Unit' or something similar. I seemed to be in there for a very long time. No doubt the logic was to keep me there in case I did in fact die for a while. I was plugged into various machines and asked endless questions by an equally endless number of different people of all different shapes, sizes and colours.

My favourite shorts

I also remember a moment of black humour when it came to removing my clothes. I had been wearing my favourite shorts. They were in a bright check pattern, and my enthusiasm for them was shared by few others.

"Have you got a license for those shorts?" was a common jibe thrown at me in reference to them.

A nurse informed me that unless I was well enough to move, she would have to cut me out of them to examine me more closely. She seemed amazed that despite this I wanted to keep them and exercised her authority, based no doubt on a diagnosis of mild lunacy, by throwing them unceremoniously into the bin. Don't misunderstand me, she did this with tact and kindness, albeit underlined with definite concern about my sanity.

Sympathy and concern

I was unstrapped from my restraining pads and belts. I don't know what was visible, but there was no external bleeding or break in the skin anywhere. I knew it was serious, obviously, from the pain which had dimmed not one bit, but more especially from the depth of sympathy and concern in the eyes

21

and voices of everyone who came to see me and speak to me.

My world had become a dark tunnel. I seemed to roll along at varying speeds, clinging both to the pain and the trolley I lay on. From time to time I would slow down or even stop, then I would pick up pace and be flying along at unbelievable speed. Always I was looking straight up or from side to side. I could not sit up or even raise my head.

Mad rush

Occasionally I would float into the air and look down at myself and those crowded around me with concerned faces. These few moments were more peaceful than the mad rush through the tunnel, but they never lasted for long. I went under an X-ray machine and then through a doughnut MRI scanner. I was touched gently, moved from board to trolley and back again, the world spinning, the faces changing, the noise endless and the pain still blinding.

Ward 17

After what seemed like weeks but was no doubt a few hours, I was rolled into a lift and taken up to the fifth floor of the hospital and parked in a bay within a ward which I later came to know as Ward 17, my home for the next ten days. It was night, I think the space I was in had eight beds in total, four in a line on each side of the small ward.

Either before or after my arrival on the ward, I was hooked up to a morphine drip. This had a self-regulating release button, which I was to press whenever I needed it, but would not allow me to take more than the maximum permitted amount in any given time. I think this went into my right hand via a fixed needle in my hand called a canula. Into my left hand in the same manner went a saline drip. Into my penis went a catheter, and in due course, from time to time into my left arm would go another needle attached to a tube which was in turn attached to a bag of blood which would

23

drip ever so slowly into my body to replace the blood bleeding internally all around my pelvis.

The morphine became my greatest friend and my greatest enemy all rolled into one. The morphine began to kick in and the pain became duller, or rather its peaks dimmed. It was there constantly, but it was now like an ugly companion lying alongside me rather than filling my whole world.

Chapter Four –

The First Night

I remember fairly little of that first night. It seemed that every time I managed to doze a little, I was woken up for test after test. I think the most fundamental test of all was simply to test whether I could wake up. I know my friend, the tractor driver, and his wife were there at some stage. Both faces grey and strained with compassion, guilt and concern. There were bumps and sounds of various activity throughout the night. I suppose the general comings and goings of other poor sods like me.

Night and day merged together

The next day dawned without fanfare or exclamation, and carried on much as the night. I seemed to have an endless number of experts of different kinds who came to introduce themselves, release a little more information to me and move on. I am sure that many of them must have visited me several times but mainly the faces seemed new.

There was one Asian doctor who came most regularly and claimed definite possession of me.

How should I describe him without causing offence? The Leicester Royal Infirmary, like its host city, is an incredible mass of colours, creeds, shapes and sizes.

More of that later. No matter how exhausted he looked, his smile and the energy which emanated from him helped me enormously, almost as if he was going to sort out all my problems single handedly, no matter what the challenge.

Names

It is strange, the whole time I was in hospital, I conquered one of my many previous frailties, an inability to remember people's names. It had plagued me all my life. I rarely forget a face, but I have been known to momentarily confuse the name of the closest of my friends. From the moment I entered the hospital, that curse left me and through everything that happened while I was there, I managed almost without exception to remember the names of those who looked after me. As soon as I returned home, my previous affliction returned. It certainly helped that, partly as a consequence of the racial diversity of those working there, there was an even greater and fantastical variety of names.

Wonderful names

Where else other than in the pages of a novel might one meet characters with such wonderful names as Merlin, Ash, Fidelis, Dylan, Phonaeica, Manolo and many more? Remembering these great names, however, implies no more gratitude to them than to the other incredible Phils, Mikes, Bobs and Bills,

Janices, Sharons, Tracys and Jills and so many more who all together became the most important people in my life for two dreadful months during that summer.

Visitors

I received a fair number of visitors over those first few days. Seeing my sons stays with me most, their pale faces trying so hard, and indeed succeeding, to look brave and unconcerned. They both did better than several who actually could not bear to look at me for longer than a moment or two before they had to leave the room to let the shock of my deathly appearance sink in. Later "green" and "deathly" were the words most used to describe me. Guiltiest of all was my semi-retired head butcher, Alan Bray, one of the toughest and most resilient men I know, who had started slaughtering animals from the age of fourteen. He, like several other brave men, came to visit, but struggled to stay long.

Morphine nightmares

The morphine began to take serious effect and life divided into two separate worlds.

With my eyes open, I saw and felt the world more or less as it was. The ward, the other beds, the nurses, cleaning staff and various other people passing by.

As soon as my eyes closed, I was somewhere else altogether. Following an unknown shadowy figure down a dark path, into a strange building, past cages of birds, in through a hidden door which revealed a laboratory lined on each side with work stations at which sat white coated people looking into microscopes or playing with test tubes. This world of darkness could only be likened to looking into hell itself. The fear, terror and feeling of utter despair were so real and consumed me totally.

Jan McCourt

Kindness and concern

In both worlds the pain continued, a little duller of course, but in the dark world I was filled with dread and fear. Conspiracy and distrust flowed like flavours through every part of me. In the brighter, ward world, I was also lost and at times delirious, but there was kindness and concern in every face and every pair of eyes that looked down at me. I was caught between the two extremes of taking the morphine to ease the pain and trying not to take it, so as to remain sane and escape the dread.

Another frightening world

Sometimes the worlds would collide and I would try to recount my visions to my specialists who were no doubt trying to share with me some delicate insight into the workings or non-workings of my bowels. I remember grabbing the arm of one and telling him he must look into what all these people in white coats were up to. What was strange was that each time I entered back into this dark world, it felt familiar as well as strange, but never comfortable, always frightening. I was certain that I had been there before.

'Leave your dignity at the door'

At the end of my second day, my carers decided that it was high time I was washed. I had already had my catheter explained to me, and raised a smile on the face of the nurse when I asked what happened to the 'other'. "Darling", she replied, "you just do it there, then press this button, and as soon as we can, we will come and clean you up". Even through the pain I balked a little at this low point I had reached where I was so dependent on others that I would spend time wallowing in my own shit. I could not believe, with all the amazing advances in care, that there was no more dignified procedure. Later, many of the nurses repeated to me the old adage:

"When you enter here you leave your dignity at the door and you don't get it back again until you leave ".

To an extent this was true, but they underestimated, as so often, the effect of the way in which they minister to their charges. Despite all the bottom wipings and unbelievably intimate proddings, pokings and examinations, I never felt my dignity really demeaned. My pride, perhaps, but never my self-respect.

These boys and girls, men and women, were there for one purpose. That purpose was to help put me back together again, set me back on my feet and send me home. Whatever so-called indignities I had to suffer and whatever they had to do to me did not matter in the achievement of their goal.

Rolling over

Having said all that, I was truly scared at the prospect of being rolled over for them to clean my back. Not scared of them, but of the pain which I anticipated.

I shared my fear with them, they smiled indulgently, like at a child, and for once got it wrong. I don't know whether the nurses who were washing me had not read my notes or whether they just saw a task that needed doing and got on and did it. I think that, perhaps, because I had no bones sticking out dramatically, they underestimated how much pain I was in. They only made that mistake once.

Four or five nurses gathered around me to coordinate rolling me from my back onto my side. The idea was that once on my side, they would hold me steady, wash and dry my back, clean me up as necessary, pull out the catch-all pad from beneath me, lift my bottom sheet and push it as far as possible under my raised body, then spread in its place a new sheet and a clean pad. Lower me down then and roll me a little in the other direction, pull out first the soiled sheet and then the clean one. So simple, so precise and for me so frightening. For whatever reason we decided to roll me onto my left hand side, the side of the worst breaks. There was a nurse best described as 'ample' or 'comfortable' nearest me on the side I would be rolling towards. She smiled sweetly at me and told me not to worry, but grab hold of something, preferably not her, if the pain got too much. I nodded weakly. They counted to three and in a perfectly synchronised movement, began to roll me.

Exploding pain

I closed my eyes as the pain exploded inside my hips and pelvis, and I screamed as they turned me. Ever so slightly after my scream there was another one, possibly even louder. I opened my eyes to see that I had indeed grabbed hold of something. One of my hands was sunk deep into the soft flesh of the arm of the kindly and unfortunate nurse, while my other one was embedded in her ample bosom. She was screaming, I was screaming and all the others were wondering no doubt what nature of beast they had unleashed in me.

My hands were wrenched from her body and reattached to inanimate parts of the bed, where they gripped as if on a white knuckle ride which I suppose I was really on. I begged forgiveness, they all smiled and laughed, even my victim, despite her bruises and the mission was accomplished successfully even if at the cost of so much more pain.

Aside from the good humour generated by this incident, two very important facts emerged. Firstly the true extent of the pain I was still suffering was now abundantly clear to all of my carers. The tale spread very quickly and rather than penalise me in any way, it served only to seem to make them care all the more. Secondly, it was clear that my bowels had not produced any evidence of their purpose for two days. The first was addressed by extra care in any movement which had to be caused. As to the second, it was explained to me that it was not uncommon for 'things' to shut down internally when subjected to such a huge trauma. Apparently to go quite a few days with no movement was perfectly acceptable.

Meanwhile, I continued reeling between the extremes of hallucination and agony, while the endless cycle of compassionate and enquiring visits continued.

New pain

Around the third day I began to suffer from a new pain. Because of the inactivity of my digestive system, the little food which I was consuming was beginning to compact in the base of my stomach and, with nowhere to go, it was causing my stomach to distend and swell. At first this went unnoticed because of its minor nature compared with the pain resulting directly from the breaks. Little by little, however, this new discomfort grew to match its cause.

The new pain grew and took on its own life alongside the first pain. It was like fighting two powerful monsters within me, instead of only one, and I was fighting a losing battle.

I don't know whether I was not communicating all this properly, entirely likely under the circumstances, but very little seemed to be happening to address either of the sources of my pain. Plenty of solicitous enquiries, especially about my bowel movements, but no apparent action.

Chapter Five –

The Pain Nurse

Does the frightening, lumbering NHS create, nurture and encourage these amazing people, or do they simply exist and excel within it, and in spite of all it throws in their way?"

I lay there feeling more and more uncomfortable, fighting my demons and all the rest I have described. Through the mist I heard a familiar accent, a soft, Irish, female voice talking to my right. I called out, claiming fellowship through ancestry as Irish folk do to and with each other all over the world.

"There's a little bit of Irish in everybody", my father used to say to me as a child, "and it unites us all." My Japanese friends used to find this thought especially eccentric when I used to quote it to them many years later.

A kind, bespectacled, slightly flushed face turned towards me, looked down and smiled. Certainly, I am not gifted in the imitation of accents, and even less so in trying to recreate them on paper, but Ruth Orr's voice and accent are more a part of her than they are of many people. I dwell a little on this because, I suppose, being of Irish descent, having grown up in what was then Ireland in London and spending many of my youthful summers on my grandfather's little farm in Ireland, Ruth's voice took me back to a place of warmth, security and happiness. Back to my childhood.

In times of extreme trouble such as I was going through, I think we all have need of retreating to a place we know and understand and can feel safe. If not, we go mad. As I have related above, madness felt far from remote to me at the time.

Ruth Orr explained to me that she was a 'pain nurse'. This bizarre description, she explained, meant that her mission was to travel the wards in search of people whose pain could not be sorted by standard means or the general expertise of the nursing staff.

"Frankly", she said, "most people just think I am a pain, but that's what I am here to do". Every sentence that Ruth utters is broken up with laughs and smiles. As I was to learn later, this was someone whose idea of a break, after spending weeks on end relieving pain in the hospital, was to go and sleep in a field with hordes of underprivileged children just so that they could get the occasional taste of fresh unadulterated air.

I explained to Ruth the nature of my various problems and in particular described the pain I was suffering and the two principal problems of rolling over and bowel movements, or rather a lack thereof.

Entonox gas

Ruth introduced me to the wonders of Entonox; gas and air might be its more familiar description. Entonox, a 50:50 mixture of Nitrous Oxide (laughing gas) and oxygen, is most commonly known for its use in child birth. It is offered to women giving birth to ease the pain of the contractions. It would really be far more effective at relieving her pain if it were also offered to the Father in copious quantities. Although Entonox can have some side effects, these are rare if used carefully and sparingly. Taken under good advice and instruction, it is brilliantly effective at removing what I came to know as the spikes in the volatile pain curve. You cannot take it for long periods, quite simply because you pass out, and so it is, to an extent, self-regulating, but at moments of extreme sharp pain as when I was to be turned once, twice or more times a day, it became my closest friend.

Relief!

Ruth disappeared for a few moments and then came back dragging a trolley on wheels to which was strapped a large bottle of gas. To the bottle she attached a sterilised tube and mouthpiece, which she instructed me to hold over my mouth and to breathe deeply in and out from. Although only momentary, these few breaths were the first uncomplicated moments of real relief from pain that I had experienced since the whole nightmare had begun. Ruth explained that I should use this gas whenever the nurses needed to move me for any reason. It could only be used when a nurse suitably instructed in its use was present.

I subsequently discovered that very few nurses are instructed in the use of Entonox despite the fact that such instruction only takes about ten to fifteen minutes. Use of the gas and air made a job normally needing four or five nurses to do painfully, doable in a crisis by one or two. Ruth examined my increasingly large, distended and terribly painful stomach and asked me various questions while examining my notes. She talked to other nurses and then disappeared for a while. When she returned, she explained to me that she was going to take me to see a man who could help with my digestive problems.

Trolley dash

My pain was mounting again. Now it was the swelling of my stomach which was easily outdoing the pain of my breaks. I looked several months into pregnancy with one or perhaps several large babies growing inside me. I was beginning to feel a strange bubbling sensation in my stomach and a foul taste in my mouth. Every now and then I would burp, and though relieved a little by this, felt as if I would vomit. My pain and discomfort were becoming increasingly evident.

Ruth telephoned for a porter but was told that there would not be one available to help her for some time. She put down the phone, kicked off the brakes on my bed, having detached it from the many connections to the wall, making sure that my various drips were not left behind, and pulled the bed out into the alleyway of the ward. With one hand pushing the bed and the other pulling the little Entonox gas cart, she pushed and banged our way out of the ward and down the corridor.

Our progress was slow and uncertain, except on the straight bits where we gathered speed. I was struggling more and more, beginning to moan and cry again with the pain. Ruth talked to me as we went along and greeted various people she knew as we seemed to move into and out of lifts, along corridors and down, I think most aptly, into the bowels of the hospital. All I could see were the ceiling and Ruth's face, her brow dotted with perspiration as she grew hotter and hotter from the tremendous effort she was making. She called as she went, for someone to help her, but no help came.

I am certain that until this point, Ruth was breaking every Health and Safety rule in the book by doing all this without help. Shortly before we reached our destination a porter joined us to take over pushing the bed from

Ruth so that she had only to pull the little gas cart along behind her.

I was by now writhing in pain and retching a vile stew at the pressure building up in my belly. We halted outside a door upon which Ruth knocked and then entered alone. A moment later she came out and signaled for the porter to wheel me in. It was a small room, the details of which I did not take in except for the presence of a kind faced man in shirt and tie holding what resembled a large pressure washer or steam cleaner. Above him, suspended from the ceiling, were a number of screens.

Horror film

Ruth introduced me quickly to the man who explained that his speciality was to check out patients' bowels. He did this by pushing an impossibly large looking piece of equipment, which he was holding, up their bottoms. Then he would look through its camera to look for any internal damage I might have suffered in the accident. He explained that I would need to roll onto my side for him to accomplish this jolly task and that images of the insides of my gut would be shown live on the screen which hung down from the ceiling. I could choose to look or not. There would also be quite a bit of noise as the machine would also suck its way as it went and remove all the rotting contents of my stomach which were threatening to explode out through my mouth. He and Ruth worked very smoothly and quickly. She moved my bed into position, brought the Entonox around to my left hand side, placed the tube in my mouth and instructed me to start to breathe deeply and slowly. After half a dozen breaths, the pain began to ease a little and I began to feel more and more light-headed.

"Ready?" she asked. I showed a raised thumb, and deftly, she reached over me and in one smooth movement rolled me onto my left side. It all still hurt as I could feel the breaks grinding and my belly protesting. With the sharpening of the pain again, I held my breath, so making it even worse. Ruth noticed immediately and reminded me to continue to breathe deeply until I felt myself fading away, then to breathe the air normally until the pain returned, and then to start on the gas again. I heard the words of the gentleman at my rear end explaining what he was doing, and apologising in advance for any discomfort he might be about to inflict. Through my hazy consciousness, I could hear the sucking of the machine as it moved inside me. I felt no discomfort, because, I suppose of the combination of the gas and the pain I was already in.

An unusual view

I looked up at the screen in fascination, as I have never been especially squeamish. The machine moved deeper inside me making louder and louder noises, but giving immediate relief as it sucked out the vileness from me. Its operator kept up a running commentary explaining just which bit of me we were seeing on the screen at any time. Ruth smiled down at me and I lay mesmerised and high with the combination of gas, relief and wonderment at what I was seeing, hearing and experiencing.

A case for cloning

Physically, I deflated like a balloon. Emotionally, my spirits soared at the relief and with the wonder of the whole process. I think I was in there for about twenty minutes or so, and I left with the great news that my guts, while they did appear to have gone on strike, seemed to have survived the accident entirely undamaged. This time there was neither the wait for a porter nor the panic of the earlier urgency. My rolling journey back to the ward was almost pleasant, so great in every sense was my relief.

Ruth settled me back in my place on the ward, updated the nurses and my charts and, telling me to call for her any time, she went on her way in search of more pain to relieve. It was definitely not the last time I was to see

Ruth. I remain eternally grateful for her particularly dogged fulfillment of her unusual role. Even then though, after my first encounter with her I was filled with amazement at the simple brilliance of her job and the joy with which she went about her task. I have no idea whether there are Ruths at all hospitals or even many of them at The Leicester Royal, but if ever there was a case to support cloning, she was it.

Chapter Six –

Survival

After that excitement, my days returned to the cycle of general distress, sleep and hazy, but very welcome, visits from various friends, close, distant, and remote. Looking back, there were people who I would have expected to be at the front line of visitors, who never came. Yet there came many more who I would never have expected to hear from, let alone see. I had no expectations at all as to visitors. I was frozen in a bubble. My only focus was on survival and dealing with the pain and the stubbornness of my bodily functions.

Cheap batteries

Every visitor represented a genuine and welcome surprise for me. I felt very guilty, though, because my energy levels were so low that for most of my time in hospital I could only concentrate on anything for a few moments at a time. I especially struggled if there were more than two people at a time. I was like the TV Bunny running on cheap batteries, bright and sparky at the beginning of the visit, and then quickly winding down to a state of mumbling incoherence.

Cards of good wishes started to come flying in. I can tell you, if ever in doubt about visiting or writing to someone in hospital, don't hesitate, do it.

I suppose I was three or four days into my stay now and there was still no confirmation of when I was to be operated on. Understandably, I had been told that they needed to spend several days stabilizing and assessing me, the blood that I had lost needed replacement. Because of the specific nature of my various injuries they needed to put together a team of three specialist surgeons.

A date at last

After what seemed to me to have been an unending time of misery and pain I was informed that, all being well, my operation would take place on the morning of 27th July, ten days after my accident. This seemed to me to be a huge time in my very uncertain future. I steeled myself to focus totally on that date. I was determined to be in as good shape as was possible so that there would be no possible excuse, caused by me at least, for putting off the day. At the same time I was acutely aware of the problems that the NHS had with timetabling surgeries.

I had the internal conflict of preparing myself for the day and steeling myself to cope with the possible disappointment should the procedure be postponed.

Crushed

The pain had now stabilised to an extent. I hate to dwell upon it, but it is a key ingredient in what I am trying to convey. Still huge and constant, it continued to fill my days and nights. My only escapes were either into the madness of my morphine-induced netherworld or to the brief periods of sleep into which I dropped at the most unpredictable of times.

Sadly my bowels had only been temporarily relieved by their introduction to the strange sucking machine. Like the well-known scene from the film 'Alien', me a far less attractive Sigourney Weaver, my stomach began to grow again. With its expansion, the pain returned, this time only worse. It is terrible to relate, but I so desperately wanted to shit or fart, or both, to relieve the agony. There goes that dignity again! With hope in their eyes my nurses would administer the gas and roll me over on to my side, looking for signs of some relief, and shared my disappointment at the stubbornly spotless pad beneath me. As the monster grew within me, it felt like some live being clawing its way inside me trying to escape through the only other available orifice.

The Volcano

As I realised what was about to happen I called for help. I shouted louder and louder, beginning to panic. I began to gag, I could hear the nurses running towards me, but they were too late. I retched and first a little monstrous bile, then a dark brown, gruesome smelling, river of foulness gushed from my mouth. It went everywhere. On me, my bed, the curtains, and all over the floor. It felt as if my whole being and everything inside me was being thrown out through my mouth. The taste and smell were indescribable and my sense of shame, absolute. Incredibly, the boys and girls who had come to help were totally unfazed by all this. Their immediate reaction was to reassure and calm me as if vomiting shit was an every-day occurrence in their lives which, on reflection, I suppose was probably the case. They cleaned me up as best they could and changed my bedding. The only thing they did which I could never understand was to leave a large accusatory stain of my vomit on the curtain which marked the space between my berth and that of my neighbour.

I remember that stain so clearly. It became an obsession with me. To my shame I would babble on about it to anyone who would listen in my subsequent moments of delusional hysteria. Yet, inexplicably, the stain stayed on the ward as long as I did. Maybe they feared that as soon as they changed the curtain, I would repeat the act, which of course I did, several times, though not quite to such devastating effect. Maybe there was just not the budget or the time to cover curtain changing, I don't know, but it seemed so strange to leave it there when so much effort was otherwise put into keeping everything else so clean.

Chapter Seven –

I Am Not Alone

From then started my six days of nil by mouth.

The neighbour, with whom I had so nearly shared my ruinous upheaval, was called Tim. From what I could gather Tim had been in a motorbike accident some four years previously resulting in a broken back and massive head injuries. The result of this was that he had a degree of both mental and physical paralysis. Tim was generally fairly quiet during the day. He received visits every day from his gentle, sweet wife who talked softly to him. Lines of care and desperation were etched on her face as she sat there reassuring him and putting him at ease. I am not sure to what extent he spoke back to her, or even to what extent he knew what was going on around him. I do know that he was often distressed, and that on occasions he would roll around as best he could and even sometimes try to break off the side of his bed and launch himself off it. He never managed to achieve this but that did not lessen his efforts to succeed.

Night time was the worst time for all of us. After dark, Tim would talk constantly out loud. Without wishing to be unkind, he raved. His ravings bore some logic. Maybe, like my own hallucinations, they were induced by his cocktail of drugs, perhaps they represented the private world into which he had been consigned by his accident. It could be that they made a small amount of sense to me because of my own, at times, insane ramblings.

Air traffic control

He seemed to exist within a military context. Aircraft I think. I believe that he spent most of his time talking aeroplanes down to land. I have no idea whether there was some connection between his earlier life and his imaginings, but he did sound as if he knew what he was talking about. It was as if somewhere a real aeroplane was coming in safely to land thanks to him. I would listen to him and wonder if in some strange misunderstood quantum crack of time he might indeed be rendering a useful service to someone.

Most of the time his monologues were reasonably calm, but eventually he would become more and more distressed. His shouting became so wearing for all of us both because of the increasing volume, but perhaps even more because of the state of extreme stress into which he drove himself. The night nurses did their best to come and settle him, but his demands were constant, and he generally started up again pretty much as soon as they had left. I remembered that at boarding school at night we used to talk to sleep talkers and very often have totally coherent conversations with them. I had had similar experiences with my children.

Shut the F**k Up

So I started talking to Tim. I always stayed out of his private world until he started to get upset. Then I would, ever so gently, start to tell him what a fine job he was doing, that he had had a long day and that it was time to rest and get some kip. I tried to adopt some of the jargon he was using. Amazingly it worked. He calmed down, became fairly coherent and generally dozed off, or if not, would continue talking to himself or his imaginary colleagues in a peaceful, contented rhythm. This would happen several times each night. I think it helped me by giving me a sense of some usefulness, I hope it helped Tim, and it was certainly more civilised than shouts of "shut the fuck up!" which could be heard from elsewhere on other wards, echoing poetically through the night.

Opposite me lay an elderly man. I don't remember his specific challenges other than that he struggled to sit up for long. With help, however, he could sit in a wheelchair and move himself around. He definitely seemed to improve with each day.

On his right was initially an empty bed which was soon taken by a very tall, large person of uncertain sex, wearing a wig which definitely had a mind of its own, and who (not the wig) spoke in stentorian tones. Similarly I have no recollection of what he or she was suffering from.

The bed to my left seemed to be very much the 'short stay' part of our section. A seamless procession of incumbents came and went. One I do remember was the result of another motorbike accident, far less serious than Tim's, attended by suntanned young and not so young bodies and a great deal of cursing.

Crushed

John

The last of the six beds was occupied by John. I think he came in on the day after my mishap. I couldn't look across to him, as I still could barely raise my own head, but I heard his calm clear voice greet the nurses and doctors with such charm and politeness that I immediately wanted to know more about him. Without being able to see each other we started to talk to each other in quiet moments both during the day and at night. From what I can remember, John was in his sixties and had been a miner for most of his life and now lived alone with a few cats in Loughborough. The morning of his admission he had stepped out of his shower, tripped, knocked himself out and broken his back near the bottom of his spine.

John lay there unconscious for several hours before he was discovered and the alarm raised. The freakish nature of his accident seemed extraordinary and yet he told me later that a lady was admitted to a bed next to him with exactly the same injury except she had slipped while getting out of a bath not a shower. John and I chatted quietly on and off during the days and his calm, polite and considerate voice was an inspiration to me.

Night-time delusions

The days dragged slowly on, and I became more and more delusional, especially at night. I know now that one of the main things I was struggling with was a deep sense of unreality. In my deepest self I simply did not believe what had happened to me. I began to hear voices. At first they made no particular sense, merely forming part of my general confusion and bewilderment. Gradually though, the words took shape in the form of encouragement to me to pull out the various intravenous lines and hop out of bed. Very quiet at first, this particular suggestion grew louder and louder. It told me that in fact the whole experience was an elaborate hoax perpetrated by friends of mine. (with friends like these...) It did not mention any of these by name.

The voice grew more and more insistent and I wanted more and more desperately to believe what I was being told. I hurt so badly, the whole story was too incredible to have been true, it must have been a trick of some kind. I reached for my morphine and saline drip lines with my right hand and began to tug at them.

At the same time I began to try to swing my legs off the bed to reach for the ground. I felt strong, I felt that finally after all this time I was taking control of the situation. I have no idea now whether I was in fact awake or asleep.

I heard another tiny voice just as my eyes opened telling me not to be so stupid. No friend of mine would do such a terrible thing to me. Wake up. This is real. Stay still. The pain of trying to move seared across my middle. I did open my eyes, my hands were still on the drip lines, my body was wet with perspiration and all my muscles were tensed with effort and pain.

I removed my hand, breathing deeply, trying as best I could to relax. There was no longer any illusion, I really was lying, desperately alone, almost broken in half, terrified and unsure of anything. I didn't call for help. Like John, I hated asking for anything, I hated being a burden, and I rebelled against the total loss of independence. I squeezed my morphine button several times trying to relieve the pain which was again battering me incessantly.

It just continued unabated, smashing into me, wave after relentless wave. Unforgiving and unrelenting. I called out again and again. The duty nurse came, but there was nothing she could do, I was on the maximum of everything. She tried her best to calm me and then was called away to another needy soul. But the pain just kept on at me until I could not stand it any longer. Any movement only made it worse but I couldn't stay still. A vicious circle of ever increasing pain just built and built. I cried, sobbed and called out for mercy. I knew that I must be either waking the others or keeping them awake if not. But I could not stop.

A good shout

John's clear voice spoke across the room to me.

"It's all right Jan, you'll be okay matey, don't worry, just have a good shout, It'll pass" His calm voice spoke to me every time the pain got too much and I began to scream. The nurses couldn't help me, but just as Tim had talked his aeroplanes down to safety, and I had talked him towards some form of peace, so John spent the rest of that night talking gently to me, from across the room, reassuring me, hour after hour, and helping me to survive through to dawn and achieve a little sleep.

The following day we joked about it as I thanked him again and again.

John spent a great deal of time with nurses and a consultant who were trying a new system of healing his broken back by clamping him into some sort of girdle to try and avoid having to operate on him. Sadly their efforts failed, and he suffered terribly. It was the first time I had heard him complain in the long week since we had first spoken. Trying to squeeze him into the girdle had caused him intense pain and he cried without shame.

That night it was John's turn to cry. On into the night he did a fair impression of me the night before. There is something about the raw pain which cannot be touched by any medical help and yet stops just short of causing unconsciousness. It is no longer softened by the dubious benefit of the initial shock of the accident and the numbing flow of adrenalin. I tried my best to do for John as he had done for me. I called out to him that he would pull through too, and together we survived another long night, to laugh again about it the next day.

Night again

Despite the nil by mouth injunction, my stomach started to distend again. I had no idea what the time was but it was late and dark, and at night, like at weekends, it was always harder to find help, especially when a doctor was needed. Again I was starting to gag and retch. This time though, I was struggling to breathe, I was becoming truly desperate.

The only solution was one where the cure was almost as bad as the cause. The nurse decided that it would be necessary to put a narrow tube up through my nose, down the back of my throat into my stomach and empty my stomach through the tube into a bag. The nurses had paged a doctor to help with the procedure, but rather than wait, started to prepare. The curtains came around my bed. The angle poise lamp on the wall shone harshly down on me. I lay there waiting while two nurses opened a package with the tube and bag, having donned yet another pair of rubber gloves. They were so gentle as they prepared me and I could see in their eyes that this was no simple slapping on of a bandage.

The tube

They really were on a mission to relieve my suffering. As I continued my retching, vile dark bile hitting the back of my throat, they tried to insert the tube up my right nostril, asking me to swallow as it disappeared up inside me. They tried again and again but each time the tube hit the back of my throat I coughed and retched massively, spewing out a little more gunge. Even these two angels were beginning to lose patience a little. For all I know it may be a simple procedure on most patients, but on me it was hell. After three unsuccessful attempts, they straightened their tired backs while I lay back, my body shaking with sobs.

It's all in the wrist

Just then a doctor came in through the gap in the curtain. He was round and brown and calm and looked totally exhausted. His face at that moment is one which I shall never forget. The girls briefly explained the problem that I was causing them. The doctor, whose name, like so many others at this stage, I now forget, came to my side, took the tube and bent over my head. He gave a quiet and gentle commentary to the nurses and to me as he began to introduce the tube. A fraction of a moment before the point at which the girls had failed, he gave a twist of his wrist and shot the tube further into me. I coughed a few times, but he had passed the sticking point and the tube slid down into my stomach. Immediately it filled with the dark brown unspeakable mixture and the pressure began to ease in my stomach. Vile procedure though it was, I felt some relief for the first time since Ruth had flown me down the corridors to the kind man with the sucking machine. I half expected the gentle doctor to say to the girls,

"It's all in the wrist", but he didn't. He smiled at them and at me and left us to continue his mission attending to the desperate night-time calls.

I slept, fairly peacefully, for quite a while. I woke myself a few times as I rubbed my nasal intruder, held in place by some light tape, nearly pulling it out once or twice. So now I lay there, one tube and bag emptying my bladder at one end, broken bones grinding together in the middle, another tube and bag emptying my bowel at the other end, waiting desperately to be cut almost in half in order to start being rebuilt.

More pain

I awoke, fully this time, to a totally new source of pain. Oh yes, as if there could be more excitement, someone had taken a sharp knife to the tip of my penis and was inserting it, twisting as they went, deep into the middle of my lower body. Well I looked down and of course there was no one doing any such thing, but it is a pretty accurate description of how it felt. I pressed my emergency buzzer and shouted as loud as I could holler. Maybe I should have laid there patiently for someone to come, but no, this was too much, this totally new and unwelcome visitor I could do without. The nurse who came, took one look at my privates and informed me that my catheter probably needed flushing. This meant nothing to me, but once more the curtain came round my bed, and she fiddled around my nether regions, injecting some liquid into the valve where it entered me to clear the blockage. An immediate stream gushed into the bag and my relief from this particular pain was simultaneous. Like so many things, this procedure became very familiar to me to the extent that in this regard at least, I was better able to inform the nurses what needed doing than they were. They won't like that!

Jan McCourt

Of the many things about the nurses that amazed me was that their way of working was totally geared towards the patient making decisions based on his or her own experience. This applied both to certain procedures as well as to drug administration. It was, of course, carefully controlled, but it gave me and I am sure others, once accustomed to it, the feeling that we were, to some small extent at least, involved in our own recovery and treatment. I only actually noticed it some time after I had been operated on. It is a brilliant concept. I am curious to know whether it was unique to the brilliance of those looking after me, or is fundamental to the nursing profession.

I remember needing help during one of my delirious nights, precisely what for, I no longer recall. A powerfully built male black nurse came to help me. I was in a particularly bad way and for some reason, whatever it was that he was helping me with, involved me seeing my penis for the first time since the accident.

Crushed

It took my breath away in more ways than one.

I am far too modest to comment on its proportions before the accident, but now it was huge beyond belief, as were the testicles upon which it lay. But while this might have in some sick way been one of the few positives to come from my experience, (this was surely the most successful method of penis enlargement known to man, if a little too dramatic to be commercially successful), what truly alarmed me was that my meat and two veg had turned as black as the night, or more accurately as black as the skin of Manolo, the male nurse who stood at my side. I don't know what I said to him, but I recall being like the idiot who once in the hole has no idea when to stop digging. Manolo took it all in his stride, however, and although I think it was the first time he had dealt with me, he knew that I was not exactly in top form. We had a long conversation which seemed to revolve around racism, skin colour and prejudice. I desperately hope that I did not offend him in any way. I am sure that we parted that night and later as friends. What I had not realised was the tender nerve I had unwittingly touched upon which I was to discover reared its ugly head from time to time on the wards. (Can a nerve rear its head, ugly or otherwise?) More of that later.

Chapter Eight –

Preparing for the big day

Time was crawling towards the tenth and all important day. The day of my operation. I certainly did not feel any more stable, but I suppose I must have been, for other than my hallucinations, my general condition did not seem to be getting any worse. The Doctor, who had earlier laid claim to me, came at least once a day briefly to check on me and confirm that we were on target for the operation. There were to be three consultants operating on me, led by Mr Williams.

A couple of days before the great day Mr Williams came to see me. He explained in minute detail exactly what he and his colleagues intended doing. They were going to cut me across from hip to hip, lift everything out of the way and go inside the pelvis and try to stick it back together with a combination of pins and what he called plates. In fact these plates each appear on my x rays to resemble a long motor bike chain, a series of links snaking their way around the inside of my pelvis, from time to time pierced and fixed in place by what looks alarmingly like a carpentry screw. He explained then or later that fixing all the breaks would be like taking a polo mint, stamping on it and then trying to piece the broken bits back in their original place. Inevitably, just as most of the pieces were in position, there would not be room for the last one, and the whole thing would be in risk of collapse. At the same time they would reset my broken hip.

The Surgeons

I believe Mr Williams to be a truly great man, as I have no doubt are his two colleagues (of whom I sadly have little recollection) who were involved in my rebuild.

Certainly the esteem in which he was held by his nursing colleagues was very great indeed. He is the only one of the surgeons with whom I had regular contact, before the operation and after. He speaks with a soft Welsh lilt, looking like he might play rugby for Wales either at scrum half or on the wing, and every word is carefully measured. He wears a half smile at all times when I have seen him. Whether that is the effect I had on him or is his general demeanour, I have no idea. In the course of describing what needed to be done, he explained that the surgery was very delicate and, of the various dangers, there was one nerve which if cut could result in serious paralysis, and another which if affected could incur a loss of sexual function.

Priorities

When you are lying there nearly broken in half, with tubes coming in and out of almost every available orifice, and you are told that the operation you need might in fact do you as much damage as good, you either collapse or you laugh it off with a brave smile and explain that you were not contemplating sex for a while anyway. I did the latter, at least I hope I did. In fact I felt quite calm. I suppose I had a list of priorities, and this firm but gentle man was offering the possibility of either achieving all or some of those.

Number One: Live
Number Two: Walk
Number Three: Retain Erectile Function

Though it was only a short list, it seemed to me that there was a big enough gap between One and Two, and a whole world of distance between Two and Three.

Now that I was only forty-eight hours from the big day, things began to hot up. The experts descended upon me again, one after the other, and many with great regularity. Although they all maintained a certain degree of formality, they each behaved towards me as if we were in a sense partners in a major endeavour, which, after all, we definitely were. They made me feel, not as if I was a lump of meat that they were planning to cut into, but that I was part of the team itself which would do everything within its power to put me back together again.

The Anaesthetist

One lady in particular came and spent a great deal of time with me. She was very beautiful, with long red curly hair and the most wonderful smile. Not to detract from her qualities, you must remember that in my delirious state, no one in the real world looked to me anything other than beautiful or handsome. In my other morphine induced nightmare land all the characters were dark and deformed. She introduced herself to me as my anaesthetist for the operation. She explained minutely the particular challenges of keeping me alive, but asleep, during such a long and arduous procedure. She detailed, precisely, the

epidural system she would use, naming
drugs and routines and alternatives in
a concentrated effort to put me at ease.
I think that she thought that I was
following and understood everything
she was saying to me, and I did manage
to ask a few questions. In reality, I was
simply enjoying looking at her, her
eyes, her smile and the way her hair fell
about her face, while nodding at what
seemed to be appropriate moments. I
simply surrendered myself then and
later, just before the operation itself to
her brilliance and her beauty. In a way
these amazing people provided the
calm moments in the storm. Their
energy, focus and determination were
together a momentary relief from the
pain and worry and each visit prepared
me a little more for what was to come.

The day of my operation would
mark six days of having gone without
food and drink. My only sustenance
consisted of the clear drips which
dribbled slowly into my arm. The only
water to pass my lips was administered
drop by drop using a cotton bud of the

type used for cleaning ears. I continued to have the occasional blood transfusion. I spent hours watching bags emptying their contents into me, panicking and calling for help if they stopped, or if I had inadvertently damaged or kinked a line. Incredibly quickly, my body began to waste away as it began to consume its fat and muscle reserves. Nothing much changed in those last days. I lay, almost motionless, fairly mute, in my battle with pain. The brown gunge dribbled slowly out of the tube in my nose, a constant reminder of the bloating and pain in my stomach and, as if I needed any, below. I am not a religious person, I struggle to come to terms with the existence of any God, Christian or otherwise who, being all-powerful, could possibly allow so much global horror, and carnage to be carried out in his name.

Despite that I did pray again. I prayed to whoever might be listening that my operation would take place on schedule. I knew that was the first of so many hurdles to come, over which I must clamber.

My children came to visit a couple of times during those ten days, I was desperate to see them, but terribly worried about them seeing me in such a bad way. Any parent of young children wants to protect them from the harsh realities of the world for as long as possible. What we all fail to remember is that in fact, very often the children are stronger and in many ways so much wiser than the parents. My daughter, then fourteen, had been at the time of the accident staying with friends in Norfolk. My nurses kindly allowed me to keep my mobile phone on the ward, and as soon as she heard, my daughter texted me frantically asking whether she should abandon her holiday and come to see me. For me it was enough that she cared and was thinking about me. I told her to stay and enjoy the rest of her break. Not really being of the techno texting generation, my slowness in composing messages together with my insistence on correct punctuation and grammar had always been a source of amusement and bemusement to my clued up kids. Texting them and others now became an excruciating task. For some reason, despite predictive text and great effort, each word took an age and a mountain of effort to accomplish. My brother called from Italy desperately worried for news. The angels of mercy, instead of telling him I could not come to the phone, came running over, kicked off the brakes on my bed, and wheeled me to their desk where I was able to talk to him at last.

Chapter Nine –

D Day

Day ten, 27th July, dawned and I was wide awake to greet it. The country was in the middle of a heat wave and the last nine days had been hellishly hot on the ward. Today was no different. I could see out of the window, a few beds away from me, the haze over the city, the heat already beginning to warble and shimmer above the steaming buildings. I just wanted to know whether everything was still going ahead according to plan. Yes, it was, though until I was about to be knocked out, I would remain fearful of a setback. Around nine thirty, it was chocks away and my bed and I were pushed gently out of the ward and we were on our way to theatre. As I passed from the ward, I called out to the others, promised John a pint on me some day and ludicrously happy, lay back to enjoy the ride.

A very young and pretty (there I go again) trainee nurse accompanied me down to the waiting area of the operating theatres, handing me over with a sweet smile. Though excited, I was also of course scared of the experience that awaited me. After a short wait I was wheeled on into the anaethetist's room to see my beautiful flame haired friend who, once again, took me through what would be happening. I just surrendered myself to her, looking forward to the first real relief from pain, even if only for a while, for ten days. The rest is a bit of a blur. Green gowns, masks, cool air, machines and tubes, bright and tired eyes, distant voices, mechanical humming noises, was that music? Bright lights... cut, I was gone.

Another world

I awoke to another world. I had been in surgery for ten hours. Thirty man hours of specialist surgical intervention, not to mention the time & expertise of the anaesthetist, nurses and other helpers. The resource required to put me back together was incredible.

I think it had all gone pretty smoothly, though Mr Williams later described it to me as one of the most difficult pelvic procedures he had ever performed. If there had been any moments of particular danger and excitement, I remained completely oblivious. I was now in the intensive care unit (ICU). It was very quiet and quite dark. I felt as if I was under water. In a dreamy state, I held my breath and pushed my slow way to the surface. I lay, still in bed, but with my upper body raised up a little for the first time in ten days. Everything seemed grey green. I could move my head a little, and I looked around. There was not much to see. The unit consisted of a number of empty spaces waiting for cases like me to be plugged in and hooked up.

Opposite me there was one other patient, but he lay silent and motionless, barely visible. I was able at least to tick off the first two points on my list. I was alive, and having tried carefully, I seemed to just about have use of my legs. A certain two out of three was a pretty good start. I seemed to have been plugged into even more devices than previously. Pulse and heart monitors, blood, drips in and around the arms. A strange feeling in my neck where something strange was inserted, leading to yet another tube. I had no Morphine button, and my horror world, for now at least, did not reappear when I closed my eyes.

Nurse P

A very pretty dark eyed nurse came up to stand by me. Oh the curse of drugs and bad memory, her name began with 'P', I think and she had what seemed to me a very incongruous Birmingham accent. She welcomed me back to life and took me through an explanation of all the equipment which was in and

around me, in particular telling me that
the thing in my neck in fact led to my
heart and so would not take kindly to
being interfered with. She told me that
I would be in ICU for a couple of days
and passed me my emergency buzzer.
We talked a little and I dozed off from
time to time. Every time I awoke, she
seemed to be close by to reassure me
and talk a little more. As I spent more
time awake she spent less time with
me, though she or a colleague would
always appear magically if I called or
buzzed. At the end of that first dazed
day 'P' came and told me that her shift
was over and that she would see me the
following morning. A few visitors came
during that day, tried to appear light
and hearty, and left fairly quickly as
what little colour I had when they
arrived drained quickly from my face as
a result of my efforts to concentrate. I
did not really know what time it was,
but that evening, I think, the lovely
anaesthetist appeared by my feet. She
was dressed to kill, I mean, dressed to
go out, in a smart coat. Smiling, she

asked how I was doing, checked my charts and explained that as the epidural system she had moved me onto seemed to be working, she would leave that as my principal source of pain killing for the time being. As was now my habit, I tried to smile, nod and agree while thinking how lovely she looked and how lucky someone was to be out there in the real world waiting to spend the evening with her.

Time shuddered and sped, slowed and stalled. I began to feel worse. As if by magic, Ruth came to see me and asked about the pain. It was there aplenty I told her, but that was no surprise. She carefully examined the epidural and expressed her doubts as to how long it would remain effective. She first called 'P' to discuss it with and then a more senior lady.

Perverted God of Hell

It was night, I think. Pain knocked on my door but did not ask my permission. He just came on in. Pain stomped around, delighted to be back and determined to catch up on his several hours of absence. Pain got on with his job without delay and without mercy. Throwing himself about like a drunk in the arms of a policeman. Pain had a whole host of new ideas this time. Delighted to find no morphine in his way, he was going to take a totally new approach. His first little trick was to send ever greater electric shocks along my body, from head to toe and back again. Then from side to side, and as they increased, he began to throw the shocks around like thunderbolts. The little perverted God of Hell stepped up a gear or two and like some crazy banshee fell to his task with great glee.

I was convulsing, every part of my body jerked and shuddered as Pain thrashed about within me. I shouted and pleaded for help, but unusually the girls seemed to take an age to come to my side. By now I was thrashing around on my bed, each demented movement encouraging Pain to redouble his efforts and the site of my operation seared deep and burning within me. Why were the girls merely smiling and calmly checking my readings? There was no fear or panic in their eyes. They spoke softly and kindly to me, but told me to be patient, they had upped the dosage through the epidural into my spine and that would soon relieve the little extra discomfort that I seemed to be experiencing.

Pain's cunning plan

I cried. Pain laughed. His plan had worked. None of the movements I knew to be wracking my body were in fact visible. To the outside world I appeared and was lying peacefully. I seemed to be complaining about something which could not possibly be as bad as I was making out.

"Hush dear" the night girls whispered, as if talking to a child, you'll just have to bear it, you'll feel better in the morning once you have had a little sleep. Sleep! Sleep!

Pain was now having the time of his life. He had me all to himself for the rest of the night and he intended to

make the most of it. Was it my longest
night? I don't know, but it certainly
went on and on forever. For hours I felt
the jerking of my limbs and the agony
which accompanied them, but looking
down, I could see that indeed nothing
was actually moving. Then, gradually,
after forever, I could see that Pain had
overdone himself, first my arms, then
my legs did in fact start to move
uncontrollably. The lightning bolts got
even worse, but at last I could point
them out to my helpers. 'P' came back
on duty. I cried out to and for her
immediately and had barely begun to
beg her for help and to call for Ruth,
when Ruth appeared also. Listening to
me they both called for the senior lady.
Ruth took over and protested that just
as she had warned it would, the
epidural had in some way broken
down, and that while it may have been
brilliant for a while during and after
the operation, now it needed to come
out and much as I hated it, the
morphine drip needed to be reinstated.
It was the only time that I heard Ruth's

voice rise a little and lose its lovely Irish lilt. She knew she was right and neither rank nor debate was going to persuade her otherwise.

Pain takes a beating

Ruth, of course, won the day. She pitched in with 'P' and another. I was told to keep ever so still, not easy to do with Pain still doing his best to destroy me before the nurses took action, while they drew the long needle out of my neck. They rolled me over and removed the epidural from my spine. They injected me with something and the Morphine line went back in, the doser button placed once more in my hand. Pain tried hard to continue, but almost as soon as the switch was made, he acknowledged defeat and retreated to merely being his previous ghastly self. Still ever present, still foul, but in some way under the control of the nightmare inducing morphine. As the two nurses finished off sorting me out, the senior lady called Ruth to where she thought they would be out of my earshot. She

gave Ruth a terrible dressing down for
her rudeness and disrespect, at least
that was what it sounded like to me. A
little later Ruth came back to see how I
was getting on. I told her how
desperately sorry I was that she had got
into trouble for helping me and hoped
that it would not cause her more grief.

"Ah sure I am always getting into
scrapes", she said, "that was nothing at
all. All that matters is that we have got
you as comfortable as we can. That's
just a couple of colleagues letting off a
bit of steam." We both smiled like co-
conspirators. She went on her way, and
I slipped into a fitful sleep.

I stayed in the ICU for two days.
Pain did his best to make my life hell,
and with the help of 'P' and Ruth, I put
up a pretty good fight back. A few
people came to visit, some for the first
time, some not. I could tell from their
faces, and despite their efforts, that I
was looking even worse than before the
operation. In some cases the shock on
their faces was so blatant that it made
me laugh. That hurt even more, but did

cheer me up. The ICU began to fill up. The little old man opposite me started making a great deal of noise early on. What was worse though was once out of his drug-induced stupor, he began to try to throw himself out of his bed. I was able now to raise my top half electronically in my own bed, and spent a great deal of time watching him and shouting for help just when I thought he might succeed in his endeavour. In a much-reduced way it was a little like watching an action sport and wincing at the impending crunch of a tackle or key movement. He seemed so small and feeble, stranded in his huge bed. He couldn't talk because he still had tubes going into his mouth and down his throat. So he made horrible gurgling noises which were unintelligible to me, but to which the nurses would respond gently, rather as I had talked to Tim in what seemed now to have been another world. Despite their attempts to dissuade him, he seemed to wait until they were as far away as possible, and then start to rock from side to side. Once his momentum had gathered from the rocking he would, on an inaudible count like a smuggler on a cliff, give one last extra big push to throw himself into oblivion. My self-appointed role as observer cost me dearly, because of the tension and uncertainty as to whether he would succeed. The old boy never did succeed in executing his death wish and shortly before I left the ICU he actually calmed down and moved quietly towards recovery.

Next to me, after one fitful snooze, I awoke to see a large man with a large freshly scarred belly exposed to the world. He could not have been long out of theatre, but he was sitting up in bed reading a newspaper. I think he might even have been working his way through the crossword. He looked across at me with a friendly smile, for all the world as if we were sitting at adjacent tables in a restaurant. He didn't say much, other than goodbye and good luck, as he was wheeled away a little later. As more and more and more beds were taken, pressure began to grow for me to be moved back onto a ward. I really did not want to leave. I had got used to the constant half-light of the ICU, its gentle, small team of nurses and the easy routine. A little like in those few moments of calm in the helicopter, the ICU was an oasis. The thought of having to face life back on a ward really frightened me.

Chapter Ten –

Ward 32

The morning of the third day and 'P' came to bid me farewell just as a porter arrived to wheel me away. Mentally I clung to the image of her sweet face, the first new face I had seen when I re-emerged to my new life. I was taken, still in my bed of course, along more corridors and into clanging lifts. For a few moments the real hard world intruded, loud, bright and brash. I was pushed through the doors onto ward thirty-two. Stopping at the nurses' station, I was left alone for a moment before being taken to a small 'private' room, right behind where the nurses based themselves. Each of these moves involved rolling onto my side and having slick boards slid under me. By the time I arrived in my new home, I was fit to pass out with renewed pain and exhaustion.

I felt terribly exposed and vulnerable to have left the ICU. Like a mole above ground or a fish out of water, I blinked and gasped trying to catch my bearings and learn the new routine. I was so relieved to find myself allocated my own room. It was not that I wanted to avoid other patients, in fact they and the comings and goings of all the people had helped pass time on Ward 17. It was more that I felt that the demons and devils that I was fighting against were best fought in private.

New faces

I had to recognise new faces and remember a whole host of new names, but first on my list was to try to rid myself of the morphine. As I have explained above, it is very unlikely that I would ever make a successful drug addict. I had heard tales aplenty of how much fun Morphine was for others, but for me I was determined to get as far from it as possible. I started on my new course of medication which consisted mainly of a high dose of Paracetamol together with a Morphine derivative painkiller called Tramadol and a powerful anti-inflammatory called Diclofenac. Once a day I was given an injection of a Warfarin type liquid to thin my blood. It was explained to me that pelvic injuries carry a high risk of blood clotting and that with the long period of enforced inactivity which I faced, I was doubly at risk. It amused me to think that a form of rat poison was being used to ensure my life continued. Normally the injection was to be administered in the stomach, but as mine bore the angry smile of my operation from one side to the other, I begged that my arms be used as pin cushions instead.

As time passed, the muscles of my arms and legs began to waste away, so injecting my arms became more and more difficult as the area available shrunk daily. I was amazed at the variation in the nurses' ability to administer a painless injection. There was no link to experience as far as I could see. Some student nurses administered my daily poison along with agony, others I felt not at all. Some left my arm bruised and bleeding on my bed, others left no mark whatsoever. The same was true at the other end of the scale of experience. The senior nurses generally were proud of their own particular technique gathered over years of hard won experience, but whether they shared their secret of very slow administration or the opposite, they all varied enormously in their success at saving me from pain, and none was better than the best of their younger less experienced colleagues. It was not until nearly two months later when I had to administer the injections to myself for a further three months or so, that I learned just how a tiny variation in technique, the slightest difference in angle of entry or speed of pressing the plunger could make the experience so very different in terms of ease of hurt.

Jan McCourt

Daily jab

Whenever a nurse who didn't know me came in to my room to administer my injection, he or she quite correctly went for my stomach. Most of them acquiesced readily to my reasoning for having it my arm instead. I remember one young girl though, who resisted my explanation, trying to exert her authority and do as she had been instructed. My arms were at the time suffering quite badly with multiple bruises and swellings from the daily needles so I reluctantly agreed and pulled back my covers to expose my belly. She prepared the injection, concentrating intensely on the syringe as she moved to my side. Only when she bent over me and lowered her gaze to my exposed angry scar, braided from end to end with bright metal clips, did she hesitate, momentarily transfixed, and then suggest that maybe I had been right after all and ask me in which arm I would like her to plunge the needle. She proceeded to administer it totally painlessly, so maybe I should have encouraged her after all.

My digestive system was still in revolt and refused to come out of retirement. In addition to the painkilling drugs, I began to bombard my system with a range of potions 'guaranteed' to free me up. Like the sellers of magical elixirs in early America, these preparations promised so much but delivered so little. I ate frugally and sipped from a glass of water from time to time. The difference this time though, was that as my stomach swelled again, I could feel contractions inside attempting to rid me of the waste by the correct orifice. The problem appeared to be that no matter how hard I strained and the contractions pushed, they seemed to be pushing against a very well built brick wall. Sometimes I would strain nervously for fear of undoing the surgeons' work, other times the contractions would ripple with growing power, entirely independently of my efforts at control. Inside me it felt as though some massive plunger was being forced through my system with great and irresistible force.

Pressure growing

Pain came back gleefully retaking his place which had been taken over by his nasty but less brutal cousin. The door to my room closed, I writhed again in my battle until the contractions stopped, and convinced that perhaps I had succeeded, I pressed the buzzer for help in the hope that this living hell was coming to an end. The girls and boys came and shared my excitement as they administered the gas and rolled me over, only to tell me sadly that, though there was a result, it was not one of which I might be proud.

The pressure continued to grow like an animal inside me. The nausea grew with it and at times I would yell for help as I thought the monster was going to erupt from my mouth once more. Once after the vile brown had erupted again from my mouth, the nurses tried to insert another tube up my nose, but this time there was no one with that special wrist action that had succeeded before, so they cleaned up the extra mess they had induced me to create by their lack of success and my body's refusal to co-operate with their attempts.

Much as I hated the whole experience, I was always amazed at how much relief was granted by the expulsion of even a little of the foul stuff.

Dr Matt

On my first day in my little room, a young whirlwind blew into my room. The whirlwind's name was Dr Matt Jones. Bright of eye and mind, he was part of Mr William's team and had been assigned me as his day-to-day responsibility. His job was to make any observations of my progress or lack thereof, but also to enquire as to how I was feeling. He proved key to my recovery, never begrudging of his time to answer my questions fully, and where he was not certain on the spot, coming back later with the researched answer.

Matt arrived in my room just at the point where a small team of nurses was about to turn me for a wash and rearrange my position as best they could, given my limitations. It was important to put my legs and to a small extent even my body in as many different positions as possible to avoid bedsores, stretch muscles and improve blood flow. The nurses were short of the numbers needed to turn me with a minimum of pain and none of us were looking forward to the move. Coming in, Matt immediately threw off his jacket and rolled up his sleeves, and stepped forward asking for instructions as to how he might help. The expressions on the nurses' faces, hidden from him, were only for me and each other to see. For a second they froze in shock, but recovering quickly they asked him to be so kind as to steady my hips while they worked. All the time, Matt continued talking brightly. He introduced himself not

only to me but also to my helpers. He
had just arrived at the hospital,
working on Mr Williams' team. I would
be one of his patients. Any help they or
I needed, any problem at all, here was
his pager number, and no one was to
hesitate in calling him at any time of
day or night. Once his help was no
longer needed, Matt left the room
saying he would be back in a few
minutes after I was settled back in
comfort.

What no doctor had ever done

As my room door closed behind him,
the nurses froze again, then looked
slowly at each other and smiled at me.
They happened to be all girls and of
long service and great experience. As
they started again to settle me back in
bed, they explained in one voice that in
all their years, no Doctor had ever
behaved as Matt had just done. They
explained that no matter how
wonderful any Doctor or Consultant
might be in so many respects, none had

ever truly spoken to them as equals let alone pitching in to help in this way.

Matt visited me almost every subsequent day. I shared with him many of my darkest fears and concerns, but also my small successes. He calmed the former and celebrated the latter and was a vital part in my recovery. I discussed the nurses' reaction to his gung ho attitude with him and he was truly astonished that they considered him to be in a minority of one in this respect. He never ceased to be cheerful and sympathetic and was my go-between with Mr Williams on the rare days when Mr W. could not see me personally, which were few. For several weeks he was accompanied by a young German Doctor who was learning the ropes who he introduced as Ulli. At first Ulli seemed somewhat baffled by the open and informal repartee which passed back and forth between Matt and me. By the time of my departure, the three of us seemed like three old friends getting together at a pub, sadly without the presence of alcohol.

Barium enema

I had reached another crisis point with my bowels. The old routine, which I have described before, was repeating itself. Despite many small successes, I was bloating up again with all the accompanying difficulties.

The afternoon of my third or fourth day post the operation I was really struggling again. I was back to some of the worst agony I had yet suffered. I strained and puffed and tried to deal with it in the silence of my little room. Finally I could take no more and I buzzed for someone to come and help. All the oral potions which I was still taking had failed to help at all. I had firmly resisted the offer of any solution which involved insertion of anything up my rectum. Jeremy Clarkson, I was told, had said for some unknown reason that a man's backside should be a one way street and I heartily agreed with him, even if the context was hopefully different.

Dylan, one of the senior nurses, came in and having listened to me, said that there really was no longer any other option. Reluctantly I agreed, begging that he use something not too explosive, and within a couple of minutes I was on my side, a barium enema was popped up where the sun don't shine, and I was left alone to await its effects.

I lay on my back again, trembling with the same pain and trying to ignore the initial mild discomfort of the insertion. I had been told to lie still and try to do absolutely nothing for at least ten minutes and longer if possible. After about two minutes, my arse started to burn, mildly at first, then brutally as if someone had plunged a sharp knife deep inside me and was twisting it slowly and with great purpose. Next I could feel the familiar awful contractions. I gritted my teeth and tried to bear down on the pain assuming that it would quickly pass.

I was so wrong. It grew and grew inside me like a live thing again, except worse now than I had ever felt before. I started to cry out, and then scream with every contraction. I don't know whether I pressed the buzzer, but Dylan popped his head round the door expecting to see me in better form, and happy as he was just about to go off shift. His smile vanished as soon as he saw me and I could tell that I must have looked as distressed as I now felt.

Tidal waves

The contractions grew into tidal waves and with each one came the burning, all-eclipsing pain. Despite all this, nothing else was happening. Dylan called in another nurse and together they tried to calm me. I was writhing now which of course was only adding to my agony because of the as yet unknitted breaks that I was disturbing. They tried to mop the sweat from my brow, I was wet right through. They checked beneath me to see if anything was happening and found nothing. I was very scared, and I could see from the expression on their faces that they had never seen such a violent reaction as this before. I have always had huge respect for both the expertise and the wisdom in nurses and doctors. Here though, I think all three of us shared long, ticking moments of frightening uncertainty. Dylan quickly hauled the Entonox bottle to my side, offering me the tube and I needed no encouragement to take several deep breaths. This scene continued for about ten or fifteen minutes. There was nothing else they could do to relieve my pain or quell my fear. Finally I felt a huge movement within me which was mirrored by an even greater movement below. My anus felt as though it was being torn open and the world fell out of my bottom. Great wave after wave tore through me but now the damn had been breached and its contents were being released. The noise and the stench were ghastly, but the relief, in every sense, was enormous. It took about half an hour more for everything to subside.

A team of nurses swooped joyfully in to share my victory and to clear up its aftermath. Ian took over from Dylan who looked around the door once again, his expression more peaceful though even more exhausted than he had previously. He bade me good night as he was now finally really going off shift. I was still shaking, but was settled down by my helpers quickly and gently, and feeling more comfortable than I had for a long time, drifted off to sleep. The next morning, Dylan back on duty, I asked him why they had administered such an elephantine dose. He assured me that it had been one of the mildest he could have administered, and that none of them had ever seen such a violent reaction.

Later that morning, I heard him being balled out by his superior for having administered the enema just before he had been due to go off shift and then deciding to stay on to see that I recovered. His sin, I think, was the overtime he had thus incurred. I was appalled to hear all this going on and also wondered what huge pressures must have been put on the ward sister to make her react so strongly to Dylan's caring decision to put in no more than an hour's overtime so as to see through the totally unpredictable consequences of his attempt to help me. I knew her to be every bit as caring and kind as any of her team as she had already also spent a great deal of time and effort in caring for me herself.

Relief and distress

I now entered a roller coaster of relief and distress in the bowel department. The first enema had relieved me, but in doing so caused so much pain and distress that I simply shut down again. There were only two milder versions still available to try, so when the time came again a few days later, Ian this time administered the next milder suppository. Sadly for me this provoked a reaction every bit as stormy and unpleasant as the first. This time I had the gas ready just in case, so I survived it with less trauma, feeling that this one should only have been administered to a much smaller elephant. Again, because of the trauma, I shut down after a couple of days so, reluctantly, we had to try again.

The third and mildest version of all had the greatest but least painful effect and, I suppose, because this was so untraumatic in nature, thereafter I began to perform more normally. Though it took many weeks for my system to approach complete normality, I was able to manage it from then on by relying on the oral alternatives.

Exploding Catheter

I had experienced problems with my catheter several more times. No one was quite sure why, but it seemed likely that crystals were forming in my urine and causing it to block. After about the third or fourth occurrence of the sharp pain requiring a mad panic to flush the tube, one of the nurses suggested we try something called a Conveen. I could not help but laugh at the name, which made me think of an illicit gathering of potcheen drinkers, (Ireland's answer to moonshine). In fact it was far less entertaining, resembling a rather robust condom with a tube at one end, which then, like the catheter, leads to a bag. I remember watching helplessly as the nurse slid the catheter tube out of my penis and then breaking open the conveen packet, and as gently as she could, unravelled it around my flaccid member for all the world as if we were about to do something else altogether.

Even she, professional as she was, could not avoid letting a slightly inappropriate smile dance across her face as she saw my quizzical grin. I was delighted on two counts, the familiar relief from pain, as well as the simple pleasure at beginning to recover enough to have even such a mild 'dirty' notion. The conveen worked splendidly for several weeks until the same problem began to reoccur. Only this time the blockage was happening in the tube outside my body rather than inside. The pain was similar, though less intense, except that as it built on the first occasion, no one understood what was happening, but at my suggestion changed the conveen nevertheless and so solved the problem.

The third time this happened, the pain was building again in its familiar way as I waited, having buzzed and called for help. Despite becoming quite intense, I was at least spared the panic of uncertainty because I knew what was happening. You must remember that I was still at this time almost totally immobile and so still incapable of doing anything useful to help myself. I explained to the same wonderful nurse who had unfurled that conveen as she pulled back my covers to investigate. As she did so, the wretched thing burst from me like a deflated balloon in an explosion of urine which narrowly missed her, but could not miss me.

Neither of us could help but laugh, and we decided, to avoid any repetition, that I should take a huge figurative step and progress to using a cardboard bedpan or bottle. This small promotion was another small mark in my long road to recovery, though it took me at least two weeks to gain sufficient control to be able to make use of it properly. Both the catheter and the conveen relied on the unconscious drip, drip of urine through the tube into their bag. Without either of these devices, an element of control was necessary.

A new battle

So a new battle began. I could feel my bladder telling me to empty it so I would grab a grey cardboard bottle from my bed rail for the purpose. Once in place nothing would happen. Sometimes I would lie for an hour or more, the bottle cradled between my legs with no result. I began to despair. That first day when I was liberated to use the bottle, I tried all afternoon, and again and again through the night, but still only managed a few small and agonizing drops.

A battle waged

My mind, unlike the bottle became filled, obsessed with the struggle to make my bladder perform. The next morning I tried again. I tried relaxing my muscles, I tried forgetting about what I wanted to do, I tried concentrating, straining, not straining, whistling, not whistling. Thinking about it now, I should probably have asked someone to leave a tap on for a while, but for some daft reason I did not share this particular problem with anyone at the time. My dignity may have been left outside the hospital entrance, but pride still reared its head ever so slightly from time to time.

A battle won

Finally, as I lay there in despair, I felt a difference in my discomfort and a slow trickling sensation within me. A few drops came and then a torrent flowed into the bottle. The urine burnt sorely as it flowed, but with the hurt came the most intense pleasure. The pleasure was both physical and emotional. The relief mixed with the sense of achievement at having made another move towards normality. Looking back, this ongoing battle, which continued for a couple of weeks before regularity resumed, was one of the most significant of all. I don't know why exactly, but it was only outdone as a key moment in my physical recovery by those when I was first to stand and then when I took my first steps.

Chapter Eleven –

Heal Your Mind

"Not just a question of seeing that your bones knit back together and that we get you walking and healed physically. We are here to help you to heal your mind and your emotions. "

Jan McCourt

Laughter and tears

Now that my internal bodily functions were at last in some semblance of working order, life began to look up. I still could barely move in my bed but now I could begin to plan a bit more precisely some of the details of my recovery.

I of course wanted some sort of time frame to work within. Though it was still far too early to give me a forecast as to the degree of my eventual recovery, I received constant praise as to the improvements I was making. Mr Williams tentatively put a November/December target in place for my return home, but his largest, and at that stage least certain, target was for when I could start to bear weight, first on my undamaged right leg, and then on my left leg which would be much riskier as a result of my broken left hip. He counted in terms of days from the date of the operation and set a target of 21 days for my first attempt to weight bear on my right leg.

Crushed

I was submitted to weekly x rays and though I was mending well, he set that target back another couple of weeks after some consideration. He explained that some years previously he had had a patient with a similar injury to mine who was a couple of stone heavier. All had gone well and he had set him a similar target to mine for weight bearing. When the great moment came, the poor fellow had set his weight on to his leg and his break reopened with the pressure of it.

Though gutted at the thought of waiting longer than necessary, I did not take much persuasion that we should err on the side of caution. He did tell me from very early after the operation that I should try and maintain as much movement in my legs as possible. A very pretty physiotherapist attended me at a very early stage and she gave me a set of simple exercises to achieve this. At the time of the accident, when I had rolled over onto my side from under the wheel of the tractor, I had taken most of my weight on my left knee. This, and I suppose the extra pressure on that side in the accident itself resulted in a knee that could hardly bend at all. My right knee was sore, but soon loosened up. My left knee felt as if it was filled with crushed glass if I tried to move it even through a very few degrees.

No pain, no gain

All movement below the waist was hugely painful, but I was taught, despite this, to do as much as I could. The 'no pain no gain' rule applied very clearly, but equally I was to take it to the beginning of pain and just a little further, no more. At first the exercises were something I made myself do with great conscious effort, and consisted only of what seemed to be the tiniest movements. Gradually, however, almost imperceptibly, the range of movement increased and they became more automatic. I spent most of my time, when not receiving visitors, either reading or sleeping, the first to remove my mind elsewhere, and the second to keep pushing the healing process. All the time, especially when reading, I moved my legs. It became as constant and as normal as breathing. I suspect I even continued in my sleep. Each day I measured the tiny but significant progress in my left knee and rejoiced in it. Mr W and Matt and everyone else rejoiced in it with me. It was the same with every tiny improvement that I made in whatever area. They were all with me, whoever they were, be it the young lad or the older man who collected my mountains of read newspapers, the great girls who woke me in the mornings to a cup of tea and my regular order for breakfast, they all seemed to, and I think really did, take a deep interest. They all remembered the details of the previous day or week since they had last seen me and noted every step, every success and every challenge along the way. This was not a conveyor belt, this was a deeply caring but also supremely efficient team of people working together. All I ever did for them was to try my hardest to

remember their names, to be as
cheerful as I could manage at the
particular time and to say 'please' and
'thank you' at every opportunity. I
constantly apologised for all the trouble
I was always causing them, and told
them how grateful I was to them all.
They retorted that I was to stop saying
'thank you' all the time and that I was
such a nice chap and that they were
only doing their job. Yes, they were
after all only doing their job, but my
little efforts of politeness seemed to oil
their actions, and I hope, made life ever
so slightly easier for them just as they
were always making life so very much
easier for me.

Move to the main ward?

A couple of weeks after my operation
the ward sister came to see me and ever
so gently asked whether I would like to
join the other patients on the main
ward. I think it fair to say that I begged
her to be allowed to stay in my little
room. If it had not been so blatantly
impossible, I would have got down on

bended knee and done almost anything to have stayed there. I think that she was genuinely quite shocked, thinking perhaps that I might be lonely in my seclusion. I hope that she never thought that I considered myself in any way more deserving of privacy. There were two main reasons for feeling so strongly; one was that I was still struggling to come to terms with my bowels and bladder workings, and the other was that I was convinced that I would recover more quickly and heal faster if allowed to stay there and continue the routine which, with the help of the nurses, I had adopted.

The main ward was a noisy place. It was mixed sex, which did not bother me, but I could imagine might be very distressing to some, especially the older patients from different cultures and backgrounds. There was rarely a moment of peace out there. There was one lady who called out in a language unintelligible to me during all her waking hours. I remember her well, not just because of the noise she made, but because whatever she was calling in, her language sounded very much like my name, Jan. Stop what you are doing and call out my name loudly. Now repeat it again and again for hours on end. That was just one of the distractions which my fellow patients had to bear.

The noise

There was another patient who would shout 'nurse!' at the top of his voice for hours. He would press his buzzer repeatedly, and when a nurse came to him, he would tell her that he could not find his buzzer. Once reassured that the buzzer was in fact in his hand, the nurse would leave him, only for the buzzer, and the shouting to start again with no reason. The nurses could not risk ignoring him for the one time when a real wolf might have come along, but he would do this for hours at a time, day after day. This man's voice and seeing the immense strain he put on the nurses, wound me up terribly. In my mind's eye I pictured him as a large powerfully built individual, his warped mind caught somewhere between lunacy and mindless devilment. For several days I wanted only to be able to walk so that I could go and confront him and end the endless cycle of his calling. Much later, when I was doing one of my rounds in a wheelchair, I heard him call again as I passed his room. His voice reawakened my anger with terrible ferocity in a totally feral reaction. I swung my chair around to face his open door. Lying there alone, in a room similar to my own, lay a tiny old man. His face was blank, his eyes staring into nothingness as he called his meaningless chant, neither meaning nor aware of the effect that his voice was having on the rest of us.

There was another elderly lady who would sneak out of bed, and walk all around the ward claiming that no one was caring for her and that she was going home. Her plaintiff cry would go on for hours, day in and day out. If these few poor people left this strong an impression on me, what must it have been like for those alongside them? It was explained to me that the side rooms were for seriously ill patients, as I had been when admitted, and for patients requiring isolation such as cases of the dreaded MRSA. I did understand, and we agreed that they would keep me in such a room, even if not in the same one for as long as possible, subject to it being needed for such a purpose. It is probably impossible to prove, but I managed to leave some two months earlier than anticipated, and I am absolutely convinced that this was in no small part because of the fact that I was allowed to stay in my little lonely room throughout. I have no idea what the saving in terms of money was in getting me out so quickly, but it must have been considerable.

Although life was by now much easier, every waking moment was still lived in the context of intense pain. I was learning more about myself and my new life each day. I remained quite confused about many things and the slightest effort left me totally exhausted mentally as well as physically. What did surprise me though was that, despite being horribly lonely and frightened at times, my spirits were essentially good.

Racism

I touched on racism earlier. One of the younger nurses of Asian ethnicity, came into my room. She was crying and asked if I minded her taking shelter for a few moments. I was happy to have the company and concerned for the state she was in. When I asked, she explained that she had been tending to an elderly patient on the ward. After a few moments the patient had begun to shout at the nurse to leave her alone. The patient hurled verbal racial abuse at the poor nurse, spilling out a stream of vitriol, expletives and hatred. It was clear that the patient, like so many others had mental issues, but the racism which seemed to lie deep within was truly shocking.

The two issues of racisim and the mental capacity of many patients seemed like two huge invisible elephants present throughout the hospital.

The glass half full

Nevertheless the glass was always half full. I was alive, and likely to be able to live a comparatively normal life in the future. I settled into a vague routine. My contact with the outside world was organised through my friend of many years, Jo Allen, who also worked for my business. Jo would organise visitors and, at this early stage try to stagger their visits so that not too many people would arrive at the same time or on the same day. One morning, after the usual round of pills, breakfast and ablutions, Jo called me to see if I was up to visitors that day. I told her I was feeling a little tired and was just starting to talk a little more when I started to cry. As the tears flowed, it became harder to talk, so we ended the call. I lay back on my mountain of pillows a little shocked, expecting the tears to subside quickly, but they did not.

Cry, cry, cry

Instead the tears flowed ever more strongly and my body began to heave with gut wrenching sobs. The tears gushed down my cheeks and I could taste their saltiness as they spilled into my mouth. Dylan popped his head around the door as he came on shift to say 'Hi' and did a comical double take as he saw me sitting in my bed shaking with emotion, the tears gushing in torrents from my eyes. He came back in and sat gently on my bed to ask what was wrong. At the concern on his face I began to laugh. So now I was crying lakes at the same time as laughing uncontrollably. I didn't feel sad or even sorry for myself, but I simply could not stop crying and the vision of myself, not hitherto known for my demonstrations of emotion, doing so, just made me laugh even more.

The laughter came from deep within, it started quietly, tentatively until it roared up from deep within me and rolled out through my lips. Each roll of laughter hurt as it came, and seeing Dylan begin to be caught up by its infectiousness, himself beginning to grin at the comedy of it all, made me laugh with greater abandon. I continued to laugh and cry for about an hour. The absurdity of it was both amusing and a little frightening. The nurses took it in turns to come in and sit with me partly to keep an eye on me and partly to share in my almost insane mirth. Eventually the tears subsided and my shoulders stopped shaking. Exhausted and not a little confused, I closed my eyes and slept.

The laughing crying episode was frightening. It was yet another loss of control. Yet it was also very liberating and seemed to purge me of I am not sure what, but I felt much calmer the next day. It was also a good funny story to share with my carers and my visitors. Dylan came in to talk to me after the crying episode. He explained that the NHS could offer me a choice between a priest or a psychiatrist. Although I felt pretty sure I was not going mad, I thought it could do no harm to speak with someone. As I was fortunate enough to have my own holy visitor, I asked to see the 'shrink'.

Tales of the Parish

I was visited very regularly by Father Hugh whose Parish included my village of Cold Overton. Father Hugh, now retired, was a gentle man. He was happy to see me in church once a year when I would read a lesson and boom out carols at the annual carol service. His visits always surprised me by how much comfort they brought. He would tell a few tales of the Parish and I found it very humbling to hear that he spoke of me each week in his public prayers and how many people sent me their good wishes.

The days passed slowly and painfully. Once a week I was wheeled away for an X ray of my pelvis. Each time I was told that progress was good.

Jan McCourt

Look inside my mind

A week or so after asking to see the shrink, there was a gentle knock on my room door. A tiny Chinese lady came in, very stern of face followed by a young man twice her height who was along for the ride so to speak.

I had pretty much forgotten that I had asked for help, but greeted her cheerfully once she had introduced herself. She started asking me questions from what seemed to be a list from the beginners guide to detecting madness & depression. She quickly came round to what seemed a bit like Oedipal complex research. Yes I had loved my Father very much and still missed him since he had died when I was only twelve, but I was neither depressive nor especially fixated on my mother. I suppose a lot of standard questions need to be asked in these circumstances, but it did seem a bit unnecessary. It became clear fairly quickly that I was as normal as ever and we ended by having a pleasant chat about trauma, shock and the effect of sudden, serious injury. It occurred to me then and seems even more obvious now, that a conversation along these lines should be a standard part of the care and recovery process for all such patients, not an exceptional one prompted only by my bursting into uncontrollable tears.

Narnia on Morphine

I could still not move beyond regularly bending my knees and sitting up with the help of my electric bed. I used a set of light weights from time to time to try and rebuild some strength in my arms, but would fall asleep after only a couple of minutes of lifting.

Nights were still very bad, and the availability of trained staff at night never improved. I would listen to some story book disks and remember a visit to Narnia most vividly. Narnia on morphine is almost to be recommended! But it makes even the best of the Narnia films seem very tame indeed.

Restricted to my bed as I was, meant of course, that any kind of proper bath was out of the question. The summer was a hot one, no air conditioning and windows that would barely open meant that only body baths could help stop me from smelling like.... I'm sure that you can imagine!

The bed baths were short, painful & perfunctory. They can't have been pleasant to give, and they were no pleasure to receive.

Hair washing was a different matter though. Phil & Phonaecia were the top team in this regard. They joked and chatted, with me as well as between themselves. They could take a degree of pride in their humble job and the pleasure they gave to me. Often these sessions were half suppressed giggles of naughtiness at stories of the night before. I have read so often of patients' outrage at being talked over, but again, I found it a relief to hear tales, even silly ones of the world outside, no matter how different it might have been from my own.

Chapter Twelve –

Escape in Sight

The day came for me to learn how to use a wheel chair. First and foremost though, I had to learn how to get into one, as I still could not risk putting any weight directly onto my pelvis through my legs.

I was presented with a banana board, a sort of beefed up boomerang. The idea was to bring the wheelchair, minus its side, alongside my bed, the levels of the bed and chair seat being level, the banana board was put across the two with a cloth over its smooth polished surface. All I had to do was to sit on one end of the board and then slide myself across it onto the wheelchair seat.

It sounded so simple but no one had thought to check whether I could sit up without the help of the electric bed. I could not. I raised myself electrically to a sitting position, then tried to remain sitting up while I let the bed top back down. I simply went back down with it. My stomach muscles seemed no longer to exist. I had absolutely no control over my upper body at all.

Being so close to a greater degree of freedom, I was determined not to miss the chance of sliding into that wheel chair. I brought myself up to sit again and this time I stuck an arm behind me to keep myself sitting. Propped up by my own arm, I pressed the button to let the bed back down to level again. Just sitting up like this was like reaching a mountain top. I stayed silent and still for a few moments, fighting off the vertigo, my carers gathered around, brows furrowed with worry for me and ready to leap in to help. At my nod, one helped swing my legs across the bed for them to hang down towards the floor for the first time in so many weeks. More vertigo, blood coursing in all directions, pale and drawn of face.

Another few minutes passed, then I edged my bum onto the banana board, still using both arms behind me like a propped open bonnet of an old car. Once onto the board, I glided ever so easily across the amazing boomerang board onto my chair. I was wet with perspiration. Hot, cold, clammy, exhausted, but exhilarated. The side bar of the chair was slotted back in place and I was off back into the outside world. One of the nurses pushed me at first, but she agreed to let me take over and I toured the ward outside and went briefly up to ward 17 where I had first lain before the operation. There was a cheer from the nurses' desk as I appeared before them a huge grin stretched on my gaunt drawn face.

I could only last a few minutes as the world started to spin and I had to call for help back into my room and, after a reverse board slide, into my bed. Exhausted, but thrilled, I fell into the best sleep I had enjoyed since the whole nightmare had begun.

Sitting up on my own wheels was akin to rebirth. First and foremost, I no longer had to shit in my bed and lie in it waiting for a nurse to have time to come and clean me up. I had accepted this need stoically as there seemed no real alternative, but I left it behind me very happily indeed. Now I could wheel myself into my little bathroom, slide myself onto a static frame over the loo, do my business, clean myself, and slide back into my chair again. As if this freedom were not already incredible, now I could also take myself to a shower room on the ward and wash myself and my hair for the first time!

I still remember the first time the nurses wheeled me out onto the ward for me to shower. I am sure my arse must have been hanging out of the chair, and I must have looked mad and bedraggled with a broad grin at the thought of such a simple pleasure.

Life certainly became a little more exciting for me. Excitement, of course being a relative concept. When the highlight of your day is sliding from a bed onto a chair and wheeling yourself into a bathroom and over a toilet, or into a shower room and sitting in that chair under a shower, you have sunk pretty low. But for me, and no doubt many others, this excitement represented huge progress for which I was so very grateful.

It meant that the next step was at last in sight. Rather, I should say the first step was in sight. Mr Williams began to talk with greater hope about me trying to stand for the first time. The day itself was put off a couple of times after careful analysis of my x rays. Impatient though I was, I was happy to wait until there was a fair chance that my pelvis would not disintegrate under the weight, no matter how greatly reduced, of my great frame.

Two trips each day in my wheelchair around the wards, and to perform my ablutions were, to me, like running a marathon each time. I would crawl back into my bed, soaked through with the sweat of my efforts and totally reduced with exhaustion. No matter how elated I was, the pain remained ever present. It seems so dull and boring to write constantly about pain, but it was ever there and would continue to be an unwelcome companion.

As I did become stronger and my chair-bound journeys grew longer, the talk of standing again for the first time became more and more serious. About a week after my first wheelchair trip, I took myself out of the ward, into one of the huge lifts, and down to the ground floor. I followed people striding along at super speed until I found a small doorway at one corner of the building. I sat, in just my skimpy bed gown, inside the doorway, looking through the glass door for several minutes, anticipating and slightly fearing my first excursion outside. After a few minutes someone came and opened the door for me and I wheeled myself out into the outside world for the first time in nearly two months. It wasn't fresh air, but it was outside air and it was beautiful. There was no view to speak of, but there was a somewhat haggard bush with a few flowers fighting for their lives. The smell of smokers wafted across from another unseen doorway. The nearby sounds and smells of cars, sirens and city life, discordant and brash like the warming up of a mad orchestra, seemed like bittersweet nectar to me. I just sat there, tempted, but not brave enough to venture further. It was a first taste, stunted and distorted, of a return to freedom.

Friday

Mr Williams came by with his groupies in tow, discussed my latest X-rays and calmly told me that the physios would come to me on the following Monday to help me stand up. He wished me a good weekend and moved on. I was that little boy being told of a trip to the zoo, a holiday or in the last days before Christmas back in the days when Christmases were special.

Jan McCourt

Saturday

Two physios, one male and one female, came to see me. Sorry! I can't remember your names and yet you were my best friends for a while, a very short while.

They carried a selection of crutches. None of the crutches were long enough for me. The male physio dashed off briefly and came back with the longest pair of crutches he could find.

'Right', he said, 'let's see if you can stand'.

I swung and dragged my emaciated legs across the bed until they hung down pointing at the ground, useless but mine. One physio stood on either side of me holding a crutch. The trick was to put as much of my weight as possible on my better right leg, but not so much as to put too much strain on that side of my multiple fractured pelvis. To achieve this, I had to take as much strain as possible on my now feeble arms.

I couldn't keep out of my mind the tale of the big man with a similar injury to mine, who had tried standing a couple of weeks early and rebroke his pelvis.

With our combined efforts I managed to stand up in a more or less smooth movement. Mike, the nurse was there with a camera to record the moment for posterity (see back cover). I look incredibly tall, gaunt, emaciated and deliriously happy in the photograph. In fact I discovered later that I had grown nearly two inches during the time I had lain on my back.

I stood for a couple of minutes, giddy, dizzy and grinning like a fool. They lowered me back down onto my bed. I lay back exhausted but elated and they promised to come back for a second session that afternoon.

The second time I stood for longer and felt steadier. I even took a few steps out of my room and into the corridor. The physios gingerly at my sides.

They came one time again on Sunday. On Monday morning they came again. This time I walked down to the end of the corridor to where the steps began to the next floor.

Talking as we went, I asked what was the technique for using crutches to get up and down stairs. They showed me and I did it.

Escape plan

Word was going round the wards that there was a new technique being tried in the battle against MRSA and similar infections being contracted in hospital. The idea was to move all the patients from one ward to another and then deep clean the empty ward before moving its original patients back in. Whatever the wisdom of the theory, I was told that my ward would be moving in about a week and that I would have to go onto the general ward when that happened. Although I was now hobbling around fairly successfully, I was still due to spend several more weeks in hospital.

I set myself a new target.

I would get out before the move.

At a surprisingly early stage in my stay, I had received a visit from an occupational therapist. I say 'surprisingly' because this is the person who finally signs the patient out as being able to return to the home environment. Contrary to so many negative stories one hears about the lack of anticipation of patients' needs once they leave hospital, The Leicester Royal Infirmary, in my case at least, really cared about my ability to survive away from their care. I had one week, from the first time of standing, to get out.

This was far too early, but I became obsessive about it. I was determined to get home, to see my children, to breathe real fresh air and to live the best life that I could.

The first challenge was to obtain a wheelchair for my exclusive use once home. The wheelchairs for home use are provided by the Red Cross. In other words, when time comes for a patient to go home, he or she can be taking up valuable bed space because the system relies on a charity to provide one simple thing, a wheelchair. In fact, in my case, the system relied on the Red Cross to provide not only the wheel chair, but various other essentials such as a loo frame, a bed frame, bath aids and other bits of kit without which I simply would not have been able to survive at home.

The Red Cross did not anticipate having a wheel chair for my use for at least ten days. This was three days beyond my target. Meanwhile, I needed to go through basic training and get myself to a level of strength to prove that I could get up and down stairs. Easy, I would crawl if necessary. Get into and out of chairs and especially my bed? Much the same solution, if need be. The biggest test was to prove that I could get onto and off a toilet. This I had to prove to my charming occupational therapist. I still remember her collecting me in my wheel chair and taking me through miles of hospital corridors to her department deep in the bowels, excuse the pun again, of the hospital. I sat, clothed, on the toilet, looking at her standing in front of me. On her command I had to stand. I knew that I could not do it to the standard required to be allowed to leave. Just as she asked me to rise, there was a noise behind her. The lovely Irish girl turned her head towards the noise. I used the loo roll holder to help me up like the handle of a crutch, and was standing suppressing a grin when she turned back to face me. She ticked the 'release' box.

Physiotherapy pool

I had a few sessions in the physiotherapy pool. This was a massive hot bath located at the bottom of the hospital. Just getting there by wheelchair was like a day's work. Deep, hot water takes the pressure off one's limbs, relieves pain, instills joy and is a starting point on the road back to independence. This pool helped me and many others I observed to quickly regain varying degrees of fitness, amazingly effectively. The short walk from the changing rooms to the stairs down into the pool was truly scary. Slippery floor, no support and little help. It was crazy really, for one slip could have undone two months of work, not to mention the potential cost to the hospital and certain agony to me if I had slipped. The relief, once sliding slowly into the warm embrace of the water was extraordinary. I used muscles that had hardly moved for so many weeks, the temporary weightlessness, the moving for its own sake instead of having to.

Not for the first time fear and elation were combined in an intense and heady mixture.

It may sound strange, but as I extended my stays in the water until I would emerge more prune than human, I would look around and visually devour anything I could see. I was incredibly thin but apart from that, with my body-splitting scar hidden by my swimming trunks, I must have looked in scarce need of the physical therapy I was getting in the pool. I was given a set of simple exercises to repeat, and then pretty much left to my own devices. I would walk slowly and methodically across the pool, a bit like walking directly into a very strong wind. At first I concentrated on every tiny movement, willing my muscles to move with certainty in the direction they ought. Pushing like this was a new kind of pain, because with each forward step, each sideways stretch, each bend and hop, came a tiny extra degree of freedom. Once into the routine, I would switch into a form of auto pilot, leave my body to do its work and look around me at my fellow bathers.

The majority of other bodies were old, misshaped and bent. Scars large and small were on show on bodies along with the fear and pleasure of the steaming water on their faces. The physios in charge would perch like birds of prey by the sides of the pool their eyes constantly scanning backwards and forwards, calling out suggestions, corrections, questions and encouragement to us all. Sometimes one of the physios would work with us in the water, laying on hands, smiling and laughing with us. The contrast between their young, toned, almost perfect bodies and our bent and broken forms was extraordinary, but, bit by bit, day by day, the bent bodies began to straighten, and grimaces of fear and pain turned to smiles of achievement as the magic worked its wonder.

My occupational therapist used her lunch break to pay a visit to the Red Cross office and miraculously they did find a wheel chair which she proudly presented to me in my little room. To witness her pride and my excitement, it might have been a Ferrari rather than the battered old wheel chair that it was.

She even managed to obtain a very thick foam pad for the chair, to protect my tender bum from the inevitable shocks it would encounter in the outside world.

I just had a couple more days of practice with my crutches and wheels. I had to agree a medication routine and the small matter of proving that I could inject myself in my stomach, just above my scar, with the Warfarin blood thinner once a day to prevent blood clotting.

I was scared, truly scared. I was pushing so hard to get out that I had not really considered what awaited me.

The morning of the ward move, I waited anxiously for Mr W to do his rounds and confirm my release. Of course it was an emotional event, but he, Matt and the whole team on the ward laughed and joked as they waved me goodbye. I was wheeled away to wait in the departure lounge for an ambulance to take me home.

Jan McCourt

The departure lounge

It was nothing like a departure lounge, but the term gave me and others the feeling of being on the verge of flying away somewhere wonderful, like going on holiday.

It was actually an old ward, full of old iron beds set up in rows and made up to the military standard of fearsome matrons of yesteryear, including hospital corners. High bright iron glazed windows let the summer light flood in and the long dormitory-like ward was a bustle of positive energy and activity.

I was helped into a new bed, no mod cons here, but plenty of soft cushions to sit up against under the crisp white bed linen. An ambulance was due to take me home, but every time one came nearby, it was called away on an emergency. Lunch came and went. One of the nurses, round and comfortable and black asked me my story, how I came to be there. When I told her she laughed and repeated loudly, almost singing,

'The good Lord was watching over you! Yes certainly he was watching over you on that day!'

I had no idea whether she was right, but it was comforting to feel the strength of her personal faith and conviction. It worried me then, and it worries me still that her expression of faith might offend some who did not share it. For me though, her singing conviction was all part of the cure.

After lunch, I began to worry that I might not get home that day at all. I called to the ward sister and asked why I was waiting for an ambulance when all I needed was a vehicle to sit in and which could transport my wheelchair. I suggested that it seemed wrong to take an ambulance out of emergency service just to get me home.

This was how I discovered the wheelchair friendly taxi service. Within ten minutes, a taxi had arrived and I was out of bed, swooshing across my banana board like a manoeuvre in a downhill race and heading for the exit.

It was a black cab with bright yellow rails. My chair was pushed up the ramp and fixed in place with me remaining seated in it.

We really have some of the worst roads and the least well-sprung taxis. I hung onto the roof rails for the whole journey home for fear of a pothole setting me back by two months.

In a flash we were out of Leicester and into the green, late summer countryside, heading cross country for my little village and home just the other side.

It was a classic welcome home, with banners, friends, workmates and family all waiting to hug, kiss and cry. The old dogs barked at all the fuss and jumped up to kiss me too. The younger rescued terrier ran round in circles like a mad thing, joining in the celebration.

All around me was warm and fresh and clean and new. It was like seeing so many things for the first time. The simplest leaf, tree, view across a field and the sky, all took on new importance. They all called to me like they had not done for such a long time, not since back in my early youth, and then again more recently one summer's evening a couple of months earlier when I thought I had come home and set off on foot to meet a tractor on the other side of a field.

Epilogue

There is so much more to write, because the recovery only really starts once you get out of hospital. Endless more visits to The Leicester Royal Infirmary followed, as did X-rays, physio, agonising exercises, and visits to doctors.

The pain took years to bring properly under control and even now still has a real attempt to re-assert itself from time to time, especially in winter.

The memory fades, and so do some of the names and stories, some of the smiles and kindnesses. The visits I received while I was there, stuck, immobile in my hospital bed, were amazing, one and all.

On a lighter note, the NHS's inability to make a decent cup of tea forced me into the arms of Yorkshire Tea.

What does not fade though, and I don't believe ever will, is the incredible feeling of honour that this huge machine, this largest employer of people in Europe, this leviathan, this oft derided, oft chided monster of an NHS went into action. It went into action for me. For a brief moment, well not so brief, all its resources, all its energy, experience, knowledge and skill were set to work, to save my life.

Yes there were all sorts of mistakes, near misses and moments of madness, but all these fade away, when I consider the sheer miraculousness of how my life was saved and how I was helped to be put back together.

At a time when it is so tough for so many of us in Britain, and elsewhere, at a time when it is so easy to fall into the trap of carping on about so much that is bad, in the NHS or anywhere else, I hope that this little book might make a few people proud of what we have. Maybe next time you are in hospital as a patient, whatever the circumstances, you will smile a bit more, say thank you a bit more and feel that same sense of honour that I did and still do. Equally, maybe if NHS staff, at any level read this, they will feel proud, not only of themselves, but of each other. Maybe the cleaners, and the pushers of trollies and mops will 'own' their job with pride. Maybe more junior, and not so junior, doctors will surprise their nursing colleagues from time to time and roll up their sleeves to ease a patient's pain, or for whatever other reason, when it is least expected of them.

The Author

Jan McCourt was born in London of Irish parents. The name Jan was his mother's idea and harked back to her Polish origins, a couple of generations earlier. The confusion which results from being christened with what many would consider to be a girl's name has dogged him all his life, and no doubt, will continue to do so. Jan's Mother, was raised on a small farm in Ireland while his Father, a renegade Catholic Priest, who had lived all over the world, was a countryman at heart.

Though he lived in London until he was ten years old, Jan longed to move out and lead a truly rural life. Following school, university, Law school and travel in Europe and India, Jan, much to his own surprise, settled down to a career in Investment Banking, working in the City of London. After fourteen varied years living through the heyday of the modern City revival, Jan was made redundant by his last employer.

Taking the Bull by the Horns, so to speak, Jan embarked on a new life and career as a full-time farmer, and built a new life and business from scratch, rearing and sourcing British Rare and Traditional Breeds of Cattle, Sheep and Pigs. Northfield Farm is renowned even beyond the United Kingdom as a multi award-winning farm based food business. Northfield Farm has its own farm shop as well as outlets at London's Borough and Broadway Markets.